HEALING
WOUNDED
RELATIONSHIPS

MARTIN H. PADOVANI

HEALING WOUNDED RELATIONSHIPS

TWENTY
THIRD *23rd*
PUBLICATIONS

Dedication

To: Mary, Mother of Jesus
Viola, Brando, Lyonel

He has sent me to bring
the good news to those in need,
and to heal hearts that are broken.

— Isaiah 61:1

Second printing 2006

Twenty-Third Publications
A Division of Bayard
One Montauk Avenue, Suite 200
New London, CT 06320
(860) 437-3012 or (800) 321-0411
www.twentythirdpublications.com

ISBN-10: 1-58595-507-8
ISBN 978-1-58595-507-7

Library of Congress Catalog Card Number: 2004117344
Printed in the U.S.A.

Acknowledgments

Many people read my first book, *Healing Wounded Emotions*. Many readers urged me to write a sequel. As that sequel, *Healing Wounded Relationships*, sees the light of day, I thank those readers for their support and encouragement.

My continued thanks to Rosemary, for forty years my associate, who has offered me her wisdom, challenges, critiques, and faithful support to write more effectively and to bring *Healing Wounded Relationships* to completion.

Thanks to Fr. Patrick Connor, SVD, my friend and most helpful editor, who undauntedly plowed through my script. I shall always remember Pat's invaluable critiques, advice, and encouragement.

Thanks to Sr. Florence, OSC, and Sr. Donna, OSC, both of the Poor Clare Monastery, Chesterfield, NJ, who transcribed my audiotapes. They were always affirming of what they heard and performed their tedious task joyfully.

I thank my faithful friend, David, for his assistance in readying the chapter drafts for submission to the publisher.

Thanks are also in order to another friend, Fr. Jefferson C. Pool, SVD, who offered technical computer advice.

Finally, I owe a deep debt of gratitude to hundreds of people, who, over the last thirty-four years, have trusted me enough to share their painful stories with me. We have journeyed together through their lives in search of meaning and healing. Because of the courage they showed in looking into themselves, I have been able to make their insights available in these pages to benefit others who are seeking an inner peace and healing.

Contents

Introduction

The purpose of my first book, *Healing Wounded Emotions,* was to help correct any misunderstanding and to counter misinformation that exists about our humanness, especially our emotions. Erroneous thinking in this area affects many people, including religious people. The book was an attempt to change the negative attitudes we have about our feelings and to give us permission to feel whatever we may feel.

The other goal of *Healing Wounded Emotions* was to help readers integrate the emotional with the spiritual, or if you will, the psychological with the religious, and eliminate the seeming contradiction between the two. I pointed out that genuine spirituality is rooted in our ability to be fully human. The book was successful beyond my expectations, so that I was continually exhorted by people to write a sequel.

Healing Wounded Relationships is that sequel. It looks at the many aspects of our human relationships, especially our close and personal ones, and tries to provide the information and enlightenment they need if they are to survive and grow in today's world. It is only with such information that misunderstanding and misinformation can be avoided.

Daily in my role as a marriage counselor, I see the same misunderstandings about relationships being passed on from one generation to another. I watch couples going into married life with the same disastrous baggage that their parents carried into marriage. The unnecessary suffering that stems from all this does not have to be. To avoid it we need a massive education program about what makes good relationships, what makes them work, how to communicate within them, the necessity of conflict, and coming to know what intimacy is about. The information I'm talking about is abundantly available today, but it is not being disseminated in our schools, churches, and universities. It will only be through education in these matters that we will, for example, lessen the divorce rate, which is wreaking havoc in our society.

Jesus became a human person. He integrated the human and the spiritual. He taught us how to be human and how to relate. The gospels are all about relationships. He, as Paul says, became one like us so that we might become more like him. He told us to love God and our neighbor as ourselves. He showed us that, unless we love ourselves, we can't possibly genuinely love another, including God.

But do you know what? After 2000 years, we still don't get it when it comes to forging healthy relationships. I hope this book will help readers "get it" and to realize, among other things, that if we are not fully human, we cannot truly love or develop a genuine spirituality.

1.

Communication

Healing wounded relationships must start with communication. In all troubled relationships, especially in marriage and family, the issues involved can be numerous: children, finances, sex, in-laws, pets. Misunderstandings can be overwhelming, misinterpretations frustrating. But no matter what may be the difficulties and the differences, the bottom-line problem is usually the breakdown in or lack of effective communication. We are not connecting with one another; we are out of sync with one another. So we can't know each other.

The tragedy is that we don't realize that one of the most powerful and most beautiful human gifts we possess is the ability to communicate. We live in high-tech times with sophisticated methods of communicating with anyone anywhere in the world; we can know almost instantly of the tragedies and triumphs that are taking place anywhere, but we still have problems getting in touch with and connecting with one another in our own lives.

We were created to communicate. We are equipped with a voice, tongue, lips, ears, facial expressions, and bodily movements to express what we think and feel. We were made for revelation. That's what life and relationships are about. We are created in the image and likeness of God. We refer to the Bible as the book of revelation, in which God is revealed in the power and beauty of creation and in the hearts of all who listen to him. Indeed, God calls us into relationship with him by asking us to reveal ourselves to him.

The clearest way to think of the Trinity is to think in terms of relationships: three persons—Father, Son, and Holy Spirit—interacting and communicating closely with one another. Moreover, much of the teaching and life of Jesus is about relating and communicating.

God calls us to reveal ourselves to him. We do this in prayer. Indeed, one of the challenges of being Christian is to develop and nurture relationships. Isn't this what Christian spirituality is about, love God, and your neighbor? This can only be accomplished if people are willing to talk to one another. Without communication, you can't have a relationship; without a relationship, you can't have love. "Speak the truth to one another in love, so that you may grow up in Christ" (Ephesians 4:15).

The basic goal of communication is revelation, not resolution. Many people abandon the attempt to communicate, saying, "What's the use of talking? We aren't resolving anything." If resolution is the primary goal of communication, we get nowhere. If revelation is the goal, then we have the hope and possibility of resolution. Most often, within the revelation one makes to another is found the resolution of our problems, because through revelation we reach an understanding of one another.

A working definition of personal communication is revealing of who I am to another person. I reveal what I perceive, think, feel, and need. Such communication can be very difficult as well as threatening, because it means opening up myself to another person. We are not talking here about the ordinary communication between casual friends and neighbors or co-workers, but about closer and more intimate relationships, especially those in marriage and family. Such communication requires a much deeper openness and honesty, a communication that must be direct and clear.

Speak the truth to one another in love.

It is with such communication that we develop trust and build trusting relationships. A loving relationship is built on trust. In our society, this is not well understood. People often talk about love, but what they mean by love is naïve and superficial, because it is not based on trust. This is why there are so many in our society who cynically ask: "What is love?" They have been burnt and hurt by someone who has too glibly said: "I love you." They have lost in love because they have never developed trusting relationships, which must be built on open and honest communication.

This type of trusting relationship means being able to share deeply not only what I think and perceive but what I feel and need. Sure, I can tell you that your decision to leave a dinner party early was impulsive, but can I also state to you that I felt hurt and angry about what you did there? The latter approach is much more of a risk, so we tend to eliminate such openness and honesty, and so never convey the true message about ourselves to the other person. The message is incomplete, and leaves the other person without some important information—that you are hurt and angry.

Such incomplete communication over a period of time tends to distance people from one another. They don't know one another and they live in an atmosphere of unresolved hurt, anger, and frustration, which gradually erodes the relationship. The possibility of becoming close eludes them. People often refer to this as falling out of love, but it really is much more a matter of losing connection with one another.

How many marriages, families, and close friendships in our society die or never reach their potential because people don't know how to communicate, or avoid true communication out of fear?

We can be fearful of honest communication. We fear rejection or that we won't be loved. If that happens in a relationship when the truth is spoken, then there never really was much of a relationship, was there? Or we fear hurting others. We have a distorted sense of what a healthy relationship is about. Honesty in a relationship will result in necessary hurt at times, but that is the normal consequence of our being honest with each other. What we want to avoid is speaking in a mean and malicious manner. Remember also that there can be malice in our silence. My oft-repeated statement is: "More marriages are dying from silence than violence." And often it's silence that causes the violence!

Jesus said, "The truth will set us free" (John 8:32). He didn't say it wasn't going to hurt. We fear honest communication because we fear conflict. Any relationship that is healthy and honest will involve conflict from time to time and will allow for appropriate anger and disagreement. We fear honest communication because opening up and becoming emotionally close to another can be threatening.

How we state things is another essential aspect of communication. Being open and honest doesn't mean being caustic, cynical, mean, or vicious. Being honest means stating, clearly, directly, and civilly, what we perceive, think, feel, and need. If I am boiling inside, I need to wait it out, cool off, and diffuse my anger before I can state my case appropriately. I may realize I'm too angry to speak with you now, so I'll talk to you later. But I must be sure to return to speak with you. We recall the wisdom of St. Paul, "Speak the truth to one another in love." Too often, after we cool off, we avoid talking with another about a disturbing issue. We let it go. We take the easy way out. This can result in our being less credible to others. We confuse them because of our inconsistency. Children especially suffer when parents are not consistent. When parents promise to discuss difficult issues with children but never return to the matter, this can erode the children's trust of their parents, and leaves children in a state of confusion and anger.

When we fail to communicate openly and honestly we not only run the risk of deepening misunderstanding, we multiply misinterpretations. Remember again the devastation silence causes. Nine times out of ten, if silence reigns, we will make a negative or wrong interpretation or a false presumption.

Speaking openly and honestly with each other is the only way I can know you and you can know me. We can't read each other's minds. We can only know what we each think and feel when we state what we think and feel.

COMMUNICATION IN CLOSE RELATIONSHIPS

As we learn to communicate effectively, especially in our closer relationships, we will not only get to know each other better, but we can live together better and deal with our frustrations. What kills relationships is our tendency to avoid communication about the important issues and feelings of our daily lives. The system breaks down, and we become distant from one another.

A marriage, or any deep friendship, has three stages: being together, differentiation, and being together but different. Being together occurs when we see all that we have in common; differentiation, when we begin to perceive our differences, when we begin to see each other as we are. We are both good persons, but are different, unique, having different backgrounds, opinions, perceptions, and ways of doing things. This is normal in any relationship. This is when we are faced with the possibility of growing together or growing apart, of divorcing or finding intimacy. It is only through painful communication that we can come to understand each other, learn to compromise, cooperate, collaborate, tolerate, and learn to live together. Otherwise this is often the period when divorce occurs, or families become loosely connected, with the members manifesting a "proper" but superficial niceness to one another. This is when relationships die.

But when we can admit our differences and work through them and accept them, we develop a deeper relationship, a way of being together but different. We preserve unity and individuality; we are equal but different. Any genuine relationship involves struggle, some tension, and adjustment. When we maintain our individuality we will preserve the relationship. "The two shall become one" (Genesis 2:24).

Jesus said it clearly: "Where two or three are gathered together in my name, there I am in their midst" (Matthew 18:20). Jesus wasn't talking only about people praying together, but about people having the courage to face each other, to talk openly and honestly, and to recognize the many aspects of their personalities and the differences that make each one unique. It is not a time when people are caught up in power struggles, or the desire to control, or manipulate, or have another submit. It's a time when people truly reveal themselves to one another. As God reveals himself to us, so God calls us to reveal ourselves to one another. When we do that, we find God in our midst!

WHERE CAN WE LEARN TO COMMUNICATE?

When and where do we learn how to communicate? Look at our years of education. Where does anyone receive a formal education in the skills of personal communication? Nowhere! We go to school, we obtain degrees, and we might become professionals. But in the area of communicating we have no education whatsoever. So whether it's the doctor, the lawyer, the religious person or member of the clergy, the person who pumps gas or works in the supermarket, when it comes to communication, all of us can be on the same level of verbal impoverishment and lack of skills.

Practically the only place we learn how to communicate is in our family of origin. We bring into our relationships the patterns of communicating we observed our parents practicing and that we practiced with them and our siblings.

We need to sift out what was good with the way we communicated in our families and improve on it. The ineffective ways we cast off. All families have some areas of damage, and some are severely dysfunctional. Poor communication, dishonest communication, communication without feelings, or no communication at all are at the root of every dysfunctional system, whether it be marriage, families, friendships, parish communities, the work place, or religious communities. Some patterns of communicating need to be reexamined, adjusted, and changed.

We go back to our family of origin so that we can better understand how we communicated then. We don't go back to blame anyone. In many cases, our parents taught us to communicate as well as they knew how.

When I observe a couple struggling to communicate with one another in my office, I can surmise how each communicated in their own families. That's why I tell young people before they marry: "Stop looking into each other's eyes for a while and look into each other's family." Especially observe how the members communicate. How do the parents communicate with each other? How does your future spouse communicate with his or her parents and siblings? In the end, the communication or non-communication you see is what you will experience in your relationship with your spouse—unless you do something about it.

Love becomes alive and breathes life into a relationship.

We determine whether a family is dysfunctional or functional by the quality of its communication skills. The two basic communication principles are: first, we need to talk about our life, our issues, our problems; we need to break through any denial of the past, any avoidance of problems, any fears that control us, any blaming, and deal with the real issues in question. Second, we need to discuss how we feel about these critical issues—like painful feelings from the past, and how we feel about one another. If we share the pain, the hurts, the anger, the disappointments, the failures, and the frustrations of our lives, we can together deal with the painful realities that are before us. We can find healing. Then we will also be able to share our joys and successes.

Mental health professionals stress the need for parents to keep in continual, open, and honest communication with their children in all areas of their lives. Such communication can help prevent children from abusing drugs, alcohol, tobacco, and sex. Parents should keep the lines of communication open to their children in good times and, especially, in bad times. Communication maintains the connection.

We read about what a great communicator Jesus was. Jesus communicates a message of good news, but notice how he also addresses problems and expresses not only what he thinks, but how he feels. As in the episode with the rich young man, Jesus is sad about the fact that the young man could not let go of his lifestyle to follow him. Later, he talks about the death of Lazarus, his friend, and he cries. It is fascinating to read the gospel accounts of Jesus as a model of an emotionally healthy and mature person. He speaks clearly and directly, openly and honestly.

Being a functional Christian has much to do with being a person who communicates openly and honestly. Isn't this part of what we are about—being a light in the darkness, opening the eyes of the blind, giving hearing to the deaf? All this happens through good communication. When we communicate with one another, love becomes alive and breathes life into a relationship. Jesus once said, "Let your speech be yes, yes, and no, no" (Matthew 5:37). In other words, let's be open and frank with one another. Let's be direct. Let's be clear. Let's talk openly to one another. Let's not beat around the bush. Jesus, in that small phrase, says much about what we are about as Christians.

A FUNCTIONAL FAMILY COMMUNICATES

A functional family is one in which the members speak directly to one another about their perceptions, thoughts, feelings, and needs. If it's a question of praise, gratitude, or affirmation, if a member is feeling anger or disappointment, he or she needs to express these feelings directly to the proper individual. When Mom tells Dad that their son John is angry with him for not allowing him to drive the family car that evening; when son John tells Dad that Mom was hurt by his unkind remarks at dinner—these are not considered direct communications. We refer to such communications as "triangulation." Such indirect messages from others can cause misunderstanding, hurt, and anger precisely because they come secondhand. These are the communication patterns of dysfunctional families. Such communication keeps family members distant and out of touch with each other, and can create unnecessary conflict and resentment. "Why am I being treated this way?" "Why can't my husband tell me directly?"

When the aforesaid John tells his mother he is angry with his father, that's OK. But the mother needs to tell John, "I understand why you are angry with your father, but you need to speak to him. Tell him how you feel about using the car." That is the mature and trusting way to face an issue.

But if mother steps in and talks to her husband, she enables John to avoid his father and this weakens the son-father relationship. If John is anxious and uncomfortable about approaching his father, the mother may coach John on how to speak with his father. John may even agree to have his mother accompany him to his father as support, but John will do the talking. "John has something to discuss with you, dear," says the mother. Then she backs off.

How many adults can't speak openly and honestly and directly with their parents? They are still relating to their parents as they did when they were children. This problem of communication originated in childhood and has carried on into adulthood. It is a form of communication that will probably be carried into their marriages.

Never presume the other person knows what you need.

Issues are never resolved when triangulation takes over. It not only leaves the family with feelings of ambiguity about one another, but they also feel disconnected from each other—and this damages the family system. Sometimes people tell me glowing and affirming things about another person. Sometimes they tell me how angry they are with that person. "Did you tell the other person?" I will ask. "They need to know." We should never take the responsibility for delivering messages for others or we become part of the triangulation. We are then part of the problem and not part of the solution.

The basic principle is this: the closer and deeper our relationship, the more honest and open, the more direct and clear our communication must be. Casual relationships may survive distorted ways of communicating, but not close, intimate relationships. Never, never presume or assume that the other person in a relationship knows what you think, feel, or need.

For example, people don't know we care about them unless we say we do. Children don't feel they are loved or appreciated unless they are told. Wives can be silently seething because their husbands don't know their needs. "He should know!" Sorry! He won't—or can't—unless he is told. He is not a mind reader. The husband himself may not even be aware of his own needs, so how will he possibly recognize his wife's needs? Each spouse must take the responsibility to identify, accept, and express their own needs—physical, emotional, sexual—to each other. In the words of Dorothy Day, "Love is a harsh and dreadful thing."

COMMUNICATION AND SEXUAL RELATIONSHIPS

In my dealings with persons having problems in their sexual relationships, I am usually dealing with persons who do not communicate verbally in an effective way. People not in touch with one another in speech are not in touch with one another emotionally, and eventually they become sexually out of touch.

So many times I have sat with a couple, helping them break down the walls erected between them by years of poor communication. Even though they may not immediately address sexual issues, I realize that the void I see in their personal relationship indicates that their sexual relationship is in serious trouble. If someone can't communicate with another verbally, how can he or she communicate effectively sexually? It's not possible. Sexual communication is doomed to fail if it is not rooted in verbal communication.

There are many people who engage in sexual relations but who never discuss their sexual feelings with one another. They usually presume, wrongly, they know each other's sexual needs and preferences. Is it any wonder that for one partner or both the sexual relationship goes flat? Many are anxious about their sexual life, but find it difficult to discuss it honestly and openly with the other person involved. How destructive this is to their relationship! Where is their trust?

We Christians believe that most premarital sex is sinful, meaning destructive. It can hurt the people involved. We are irresponsible toward our sexuality when we treat it casually before a genuine emotional relationship has developed. When sexual relationships are entered into prematurely, they often give one the illusion of being a deep and serious relationship. However, within a period of time, as that relationship deteriorates, as it often does, we hear people saying, "I thought I was in love. I thought he or she loved me." We can come to the realization of love in our lives only when we are able to sit down with one another and speak openly and honestly to each other. Then we share deeply one another's world and worldview. Then, in the pain and joy of such communication, many illusions can be dissipated. Then we are truly able to relate sexually.

In marriage, if there is no personal relationship and meaningful and penetrating communication, the sexual relationship will soon find itself weakened, less satisfying, or dying completely. Often married couples go through the motions of having sex, but do not have an emotionally satisfying sexual relationship. Wives are the first to acknowledge this, but husbands eventually come to the same realization. It has often been said, "Men express affection in order to obtain sex and women give sex in order to receive affection." Why can't it be both? It can, but that requires communication.

How We Communicate

How we communicate with one another is also of the utmost importance. The words we choose, our tone of voice, can both hinder or enhance the message. Even the time and place of communicating can be significant factors. Also, if we fail to attach the appropriate feelings to a statement, such as: "I am really hurt by what you said," we probably won't be credible. People will miss the point we want to make because there is no emotional tone to our words. They are flat. On the other hand, if we overreact emotionally with, say, rage and hostile comments, we will cause others unnecessary pain and they will become defensive. They will not really hear the message we are attempting to convey. In turn, they may either overreact or flee.

Of course, if I remain silent and unresponsive to the anger and pain another expresses, I will probably leave the other confused, angry, frustrated, and hurt because of my apparent insensitivity or seeming indifference. The possibilities of misinterpretations can be endless. Nine times out of ten, silence will be interpreted in a negative manner by the other person, even though I don't mean to be negative. This silence can signal emotional neglect by which the silent person fails to respond to the emotional needs of the other. Sometimes keeping silent can be a cruel way of getting back at another person. Some people in close relationships use silence very effectively—but also quite destructively. There is nothing more aggravating or frustrating than a person who is unresponsive to a very important message conveyed by another. It's a classic way of being passive-aggressive.

Communicating with "I" Statements

Another important skill in communicating involves using "I" or "we" statements. Simple as it may seem, the effectiveness of "I" statements can be remarkable. Like any other form of human development, communication is an art that requires speaking skills. Communication studies show that speaking in "I" statements is always more effective than using "you" statements. People on the receiving end of "you" statements can feel under attack and become defensive; they can tend to block out what they are hearing and become taken up with defending themselves or with preparing a rebuttal.

"I" statements, on the other hand, tend to sensitize the other person to what I am thinking and feeling. "I" signifies a sense of identity, of being in control of oneself, of taking responsibility for what one is expressing and feeling. For example, "I resent your reading the newspaper when I am trying to speak to you and I need you to listen to me." These "I" statements help others to focus on us instead of getting ready to defend themselves. "I" statements are non-threatening.

Even if another states they don't care what you think and feel, by communicating you are still making yourself known in an effective way and you are more likely to have some impact on the other person. Often we cop out of communicating by saying that our message will have no effect on the other person. We forget that we need to say what we think and feel *for our own self-respect,* and, secondly, others need to hear what we have to say, even though they are resistant to it. In the end we will feel a sense of satisfaction for being assertive and honest.

Notice how frequently Jesus speaks in "I" statements. "I am the way. I am the truth. I am the life." "I and the Father are one." "I am the resurrection." Jesus' "I" statements not only indicate his strong sense of identity about himself but also his confidence in the message he conveys.

When we speak in "I" statements, we convey a sense of our own identity, of knowing who we are, by telling another what we think and feel and need. We convey a sense of self-confidence, self-worth, and self-esteem. Using "I" statements signals that we are taking responsibility for what we feel, think, and need without blaming anyone else, as we acknowledge ownership of our words. By using "I" statements, I can sensitize the other person to my hurts and anger and frustration, which is the goal of effective communication.

Whether the other person agrees with me or not is not the issue. The issue here is that the person comes to know what we think and feel. Such a way of speaking is not a panacea, but it certainly can be very effective over a period of time. Maybe immediate effects will not be seen, but in due time we may be able to convince another of what we are feeling.

The only person that I can change is myself.

We can never change others. To attempt this is an exercise in futility. But there is always the possibility that we can, in some way, influence another person and make them more aware of us. Being alive means believing in the possibility that life can be different—that is, if we are willing to work at it and to remember that God is always working with us in our human condition. But God usually so works when we work along with him by doing our share. By communicating effectively, we give the Holy Spirit a setting to work in.

The only person that I can change in any relationship is myself. When I speak with less confusion and more skill, I am changing my pattern of relating to another person. I'm speaking, not in the old broken-down patterns that were ineffective, but in new modes, which leave the other person with the realization that he must choose another, more mature and effective way of responding to me. I believe that there is no greater means of bringing about change in relationships than by changing our way of communicating. This happens when we discard the ways of childhood, those old, ineffective, and even destructive forms of communicating we learned in our families.

The person I am trying to communicate with may counter by saying, "I don't care what you think and feel." That's a way of blocking out your message. The other person is threatened. But the message has been sent, and I believe that even if the message is ignored by the other person, it's now out in the open. The point has been made. The seed has been sown. Remember, "Some seed will fall on rocky ground, but some on fertile soil and bear fruit" (Luke 8:6, 8).

Remember, we said that the first goal of communication is revelation, not resolution. In other words, we need to get things out in

We need to get things out in the open.

the open. We don't want to get caught in the old trap of avoidance by saying, "What's the use of talking to that person? It doesn't matter what I say. It's not going to change him." Often that can be a cop-out on our part. Fear can be controlling us. We need to realize that my revelation is what counts. How the other person receives or rejects my message is secondary. This is where so many people go astray. They see the primary goal of their message as changing the other person, but the first goal is my responsibility to convey the message. If I do, I will feel satisfied because I have passed on my message with a sense of dignity and self-respect. Sure there is the risk of frustration, and the realization that the relationship may not get better and may even get worse! However, the greater damage done to myself and the other person is if I have failed to convey my message openly and honestly.

Changing our way of communicating, becoming more skillful and effective at it, is the first way we can really and truly change ourselves and possibly influence our relationships for the better. When we change, for instance, our sarcastic way of speaking to a more respectful way, the chances for improvement in our relationships are dramatically increased. I have seen many marriages improve because one spouse developed a healthy and honest way of communicating. The other spouse eventually abandoned the old damaging patterns of speaking. Co-dependent cycles of communicating are broken when one person breaks out of the cycle.

God describes himself in Scripture as a revealing God. Indeed, Jesus was the self-revelation of God. Removing our masks can be very threatening, not only to ourselves, but to those to whom we are revealing ourselves. Self-revelation requires a tremendous amount of trust—but it is the only way, in spite of the risks, that we can possibly develop trusting relationships.

Even mothers with young babies are encouraged to speak to them as much as possible. The mother may be occupied doing laundry or cooking, but her having, at the same time, an ongoing conversation with the child is a bonding experience. The child feels cared for, loved, wanted. The basic foundation of trust is established. The child learns to trust its mother, but it also begins to trust itself. Erik Erikson describes this trust as the first basic stage of human psychosocial development and as the foundation of a healthy personality. It all starts in the arms of a mother or father in dialogue with each other and with their child.

The kind of communication I am talking about does not mean prattling on with another about the inanities of life or the weather. We can either talk on and on with one another and really never have any substantial conversation or we can communicate deeply by revealing our inner world to one another. We have all noticed a couple in a restaurant eating a meal together, but never saying a word to each other. It is a sad spectacle. When people share a meal together, it is the opportunity to share themselves.

Two people who have shared deeply with one another can often sit in silence together quite contentedly because they are bonded emotionally. They are secure with one another, not distant. They trust one another. Their silence is quality silence. But for two people who seldom share deeply with one another such silence is an empty silence, in which fear and a sense of alienation are just below the surface.

SELF-COMMUNICATION

If we are to be effective communicators, we must also be good at communicating with ourselves. We do a lot of talking to ourselves although we are not always aware of it. It is important to realize this if we are to know ourselves. We need to ask ourselves whether or not we are aware of what is going on in our inner world: our thoughts, attitudes, needs, but especially the whole gamut of our feelings. There are also memories of the past, of hurts, of the joys of our lives: are we aware of these? If we are, we can communicate deeply with others. More often, people are out of touch with themselves. They're not sure what their opinions and ideas are about what is going on inside them. They may be able to describe themselves, in general, as feeling bad or upset, but they can't identify the specific feelings of hurt, anger, disappointment, or fear.

Within us, there is often what I call negative tapes that play twisted and distorted statements carried along since childhood. They are often erroneous and always destructive. They control us. Are we aware of such negative thoughts as: "You're a failure." "You can't do this." "You're not likable." "No one loves you." and so forth? When such tapes continue to play, they can be paralyzing and generate feelings of guilt, worthlessness, high anxiety, and low self-esteem. These feelings, in turn, generate more negative thinking about ourselves, and the vicious cycle continues on.

We can break the cycle by, first, changing our thinking. Dr. David D. Burns' book on depression, entitled *Feeling Good*, deals specifically with this problem, and indicates that, if we wish to feel better, we need to begin to change how we think about and perceive ourselves. How I think about myself can be changed immediately, although distorted or twisted, sick feelings will take much longer to heal. They need to be confronted and challenged by new and valid statements about myself.

For a while, I will be living in tension between my thinking, which is proclaiming good things about myself, and my negative feelings. We need to always be in touch with our feelings, no matter how distorted they may be, and we need to attempt to understand their origins. The more we can sort them out, the more likely we will be able to reason more clearly and make sound decisions about life. That's one of the valuable purposes of healthy communication and of counseling. They help us resolve and understand our unhealthy feelings.

I stress this *inner* communication as a vital aspect of our ability to communicate with others. If we think and feel badly about ourselves, we need to be able to convey this to another in order to bring about healing. This is what takes place in counseling or in sharing with a trusted friend. In other words, we need to have the courage and trust to share our inner world with another.

When we have a mixed-up inner communication system, we can't communicate with others effectively because we are either being too defensive (we blame them or misinterpret what they are saying), or we are too submissive or compliant with the other. The latter happens because we desperately want to be accepted and liked, and we fear rejection. So we become too confused to communicate effectively.

Being in touch with our inner selves is essential to communicating with others. That's one of the reasons many men are poor communicators in their personal relationships. They are often not in touch with their inner world. The non-communicating husband is the cause of much of the depression, frustration, and emptiness many married women experience. This also explains the way some women get over-involved with their children, with women friends, or with causes. It is a way to deal with the frustration of having an uncommunicative husband. The books, *You Just Don't Understand* by Deborah Tanner and *Men are from Mars, Women are from Venus* by John Gray expand on the skills of communication between men and women.

Why do wives allow their husbands to get away with this from the start? They often think that these men will change along the way—a false supposition. There will be no possibility of change unless there is a concerted effort on the part of women to state strongly and clearly their need for communication, and their frustration with the silence of their husbands. Therein lies the possibility that men may be influenced or forced to change their silent behavior. A woman needs to be careful before her wedding day, that her possible future husband, whom she loves and reveres as "the strong, silent type" may simply be incapable or unwilling to communicate at all. If so, don't marry him! Deborah Tanner, in her book *You Just Don't Understand*, describes the great difference between male and female ways of communication. She writes about how men speak from their outer world and women from their inner world; about how men are caught up in what their status in life is, whereas women are interested in relating. And all this begins in childhood in the way boys and girls are reared. Communicating between the sexes requires work and understanding.

Our words have a creative power. We bring healing and sanctification into our relationships when we share our words. From the seeds of our communication spring the hopes of a better relationship with others and God. When we express our thoughts and feelings in our words to one another, we breathe life into our relationships. This is called intimacy. Such intimacy can only be generated in our significant relationships by ceaseless efforts on our part to communicate well.

2.

Listening

If communication is the skill by which we reveal ourselves to one another, then listening is an art by which we open ourselves to the revelations of others. Listening means getting in touch with another, entering their world. As difficult as speaking openly and honestly can be for us, listening can be even more demanding. Communication requires skill, honesty, and practice, while listening requires attentiveness and patience. Listening can be very healing, especially when one really hears the pain and needs of another.

Listening demands intense emotional focus and eye contact with another person. It requires that we understand what others are saying, but above all, what they are feeling. Whether they describe their feelings or not, we need to be able to identify what they are feeling.

Let's talk about some of the skills that make us good listeners. The psalmist says, in Psalm 135, "having ears, they do not hear." We can hear, but do we really listen to the other person? Are we really in touch? Have we tried to enter the depths of their souls? Or are we peripherally present, or perhaps blocking them out. Listening, or the lack of it, can make or break a relationship. If we really want to distance a person emotionally from us, or be uncaring or insensitive, all we have to do is to tune them out.

I believe the first requirement for being a genuine and effective listener is the ability to be in touch with our own inner world. What are our thoughts, our attitudes—above all, our feelings? We need a connectedness with and an awareness of our inner selves. In other words, are we truly able to listen to ourselves? If I don't listen to myself, how can I possibly listen to you? If I am not in touch with my inner world, how can I be in touch with *your* inner world? This listening to myself is an absolute necessity. Without it I'll not be able to probe the depths of another person. Yes, I can hear, but hearing alone is not listening. If I can't handle my own angry feeling, how can I possibly be comfortable with someone else's? I can't be in touch with what that person is truly saying and above all, feeling.

Being aware of what we are feeling means being able to identify specific feelings within ourselves. We often claim that we are upset, but what does that mean? Can we identify precisely such feelings as hurt, anger, sadness, or disappointment? That is why, in the case of so many marital problems, it is necessary to help each spouse to name, claim, and frame what they are feeling. Only then they can reveal to the other what they are feeling.

Sometimes we hear and know what a person is saying, but we are not in touch with what they are feeling. This is a sign of incomplete listening. This is why so many relationships are superficial and never grow stronger. People are really not connecting. They don't know how to do it or they don't want that type of involvement with another.

When we listen to others, we need to help them sort out and identify their feelings by asking them what they are feeling, and then by reflecting back to them what we think we hear them saying. For example, if I say to another to whom I am listening, "Your sister really did hurt you badly by her sarcastic remarks," then that person will realize I have truly been listening. The person in pain feels connected, feels your caring, and realizes you are truly walking in their shoes. We call this empathy. It is not just counselors who need to practice empathy; all of us do if we are to be in tune with others.

Listening means focusing all our attention and energy on the other. Our body language can show that we are there, present, for the other. Our eyes are focused on that person. Such listening is responsive and reflective. We are not just sitting there like mannequins. We reflect back the others' feelings and thoughts. We echo their joy. We are shocked when they are shocked, angry when they are angry, sad with their sadness. We don't give them intellectual answers or advice right away, or tell them of similar experiences we've had. They're not really interested in those responses at that point. They need us to be there for and with them. This type of listening without interrupting requires much discipline, so that we stay focused on the other person.

Notice what a compassionate, sensitive listener Jesus is. He listened to the cries of the blind person, of the anxious woman with the hemorrhage who touched his garment, of the widow who was grieving for her son. This listening Jesus is a sensitive Jesus who was emotionally in touch with himself and with others. Only then did he physically touch them; only then did he heal them. Power went forth from him. When we listen to people, power goes forth from us too, the power to heal. We, like Jesus, can heal by practicing active, reflective, and compassionate listening.

Being a good listener means not only listening as others speak, but being comfortable with their silences, tears, painful groans, or emotional outbursts, which can be laced with irrational threats aimed at another person. There may be threats of running away or even of suicide. This sort of thing can be scary and can almost overwhelm us. But allowing people to vent pent-up feelings will help diffuse them, will bring people back to reality.

We need to check ourselves and be careful we don't disregard what others are saying by responding, "Oh, you don't do that" or "You won't do that." In most cases, of course, they won't. But they need to express their rage, their despair, the pain they feel within.

Hurting persons are very sensitive to how we are reacting and responding and to whether we are genuinely with them. If they sense this, they're able to trust us more and surface their deeper feelings, fears, and anxieties, hopelessness, and confusion. If we can stay with them, listening, they will probably reveal the deeper stories they feel within themselves.

Listening means focusing our attention and energy on the other.

We see in those we have listened to that gospel healing—the blind see, the deaf hear, the lame walk—just because we have listened. How often people are able to get on with their own lives again. How often we have heard people who have told their painful stories to us, say afterward, "Thanks for listening. Thanks for your help." We think we did nothing more than listen. But what a gift that is! It is this type of genuine, penetrating listening that touches the center of the storm in people's hearts and calms them down.

How often husbands have said to me that they feel helpless and inadequate when trying to deal with their wife's depression or anxiety. These men get caught up in the male hang-up—they have to do something to take this pain away from their wife, to fix it, to make it better. I am always reassuring husbands that the only thing they need to do, the most effective thing they can do, is to listen to their wives. Let them cry, rage, tell their story, express their feelings—and healing will happen! Cherished moments of closeness will often then occur.

Healing will never really take place in our society, or in our churches, until we start to listen to one another. Much of counseling basically involves helping people by listening to them, to what they really said, how they really felt, and then helping them to sort it all out, to put it into perspective, to integrate it into their lives—all of which brings healing of the spirit.

The art of listening is just that, an art. It requires practice and much effort, but the art can be developed. It can be learned. It requires a concerted and concentrated effort on our part. We will be amazed at the results the art of listening brings to others and to our relationships.

Listening helps us to gain insight into another person.

We must know our limitations, that is, how long we can listen and when we can't listen anymore. We need to realize when we need a break from listening and rejuvenate ourselves so we can go back to listening again. People know when we aren't listening. As much as we think they're out of it, they will say, "You're not listening." Many times my clients have said to me, "What's wrong? You don't seem to be listening." Human frailty, fatigue, human distractions occur, and are understandable. Still these people in front of us, who we sometimes feel are "out of it," are sensitive to the fact that we are not listening.

Good listening leads to healing because it shows the listener cares. Hurting people often feel bad about themselves. Listening to them binds up their wounds by pouring on them oil of compassion, tenderness, and warmth. Listening leads to healing because it gives permission to hurting people to speak about what is gnawing away at them or stuck inside them. There are few things more destructive for humans and their relationships than buried anger and hurt, guilt and shame, and all the other tumultuous feelings that are buried but need to be resolved. These can be resolved by being spoken about openly and honestly to a trusted listener.

By divulging their inner turmoil, people begin to sort things out. When we can express what's going on inside us we can visualize what is hidden in the darkness and bring it into the light, into perspective, and develop a better understanding of it. Vision and hope follow. Hope says that things can be different. Christian hope says that things can be different because God is working along with us, because God works with us when we work through the issues of life.

Listening heals relationships because, when we listen to one another, we dispel many of the misunderstandings and misinterpretations that have accrued between us and that are the cause of so much dysfunction in marriages and families. Such dysfunction is not so much in the problems that exist in these marriages and families, but in the fact that the men and women in these marriages and families have not been able to speak to one another about what they think and what they feel. That's why the formula that fits dysfunction is: We didn't talk, so we didn't feel, so we didn't trust. And if we didn't talk, then we certainly didn't listen, except to the sounds of silence, which generated only more confusion and pain and misunderstanding and a sense of being misunderstood.

There are other kinds of silence. Silence can be a sign of neurotic introspection, creating a deliberate barrier between oneself and others. It can be a weapon of noncooperation. It can be a sign to indicate disapproval or indifference. It can be a measure of discomfort, as when two people shuffle uneasily in each other's company and fish wildly for words. It can be a sign of incomprehension, unwillingness, anger, disbelief. It can be the result of terror or unkindness (Sean Dunne, *The Road to Silence*).

Listening is a learning experience, because we come to a better understanding and knowledge not only of other people, but of ourselves. I often say of myself that I am constantly in therapy, because, as a therapist, the more I listen and get in touch with others, the more I am listening and getting in touch with myself.

Listening helps us know who the other person really is. The old Greek saying, "Know yourself" is really the beginning of all wisdom and of a deep spirituality. But if knowing self takes time and effort, then knowing another person takes even more time and effort.

Remember the biblical term for sexual relations is "to know." It describes much more than a physical relationship. It means knowing another person intimately, to be close to that person. Knowing and listening result in intimacy. Some people engage in sexual contact without intimacy. Such behavior destroys one's capacity to love. For people to open up and share the gift of themselves takes a willingness to risk and trust. We hold dearly what a person discloses to us and we treasure these disclosures and keep them in confidence. We respect people for what they have disclosed to us, even though we may not agree with them.

What I share with you in these pages I have learned from listening to many people. Listening helps us gain insight into another person, to know that person, to understand him and to help him understand and know himself. Listening is a part of loving. Only after I have truly listened to a person can I genuinely begin to love him. Only then can

I accept him as he is and love him. I can say: "I love you as you are, as I know you, not as I think you are or should be."

Listening is a part of living. It means being in touch with the realities around us. Being in touch with reality is what makes for good mental health, as painful as that reality may sometimes be. To be fully alive and vibrant is to listen intently to the world around us to learn about life and appreciate it.

Listening often involves laughing. This means we are in touch with the ridiculousness and the incongruities of life. Because we can laugh with people, and not at them, after we have truly listened to them, we know people are healing and getting better because they have begun to laugh at themselves, and we with them. Humor helps us to put life in perspective, eliminates the distortions that we perceive, lightens the burden of living, and reduces stress. Humor is probably the least-used therapeutic skill in counseling as well as in living!

In my waiting room I have four scrapbooks filled with cartoons I have gathered over the past fifteen years. They are cartoons that are pertinent to people's lives, especially to marriage and the family, and to our human foibles. It's interesting to see that the young and the old gravitate to these scrapbooks again and again. They often remark how relaxing looking at these cartoons can be. God must have some sense of humor or else how could he have put up with us for as long as he has?

Listening means letting go of ourselves. When we listen to others, we get out of ourselves, our self-centered world. We reach out and touch other people. We get in touch with their pain and sorrow. We begin to understand what another aspect of life is about. As the Christian tradition says, "When we lose ourselves, we find ourselves."

When we listen intently to others' problems—their pain, their sorrow, their hurt, their losses—our own problems don't seem to be so bad. We're able to put our own issues in proper perspective. When I listen day after day to other people's problems, mine don't seem to be so terrible. I put them in perspective and then I can cope better with them.

When others hurt us and seek forgiveness, we have to listen to their story, as to why whatever happened happened, and thus gain understanding. Then we can let go of our hurt, anger, and pain. We can forgive because we understand.

Listening means letting go of ourselves.

These are some of my own personal reflections on listening, gained from listening to others. I'm sure in your own listening, you have learned many other aspects of wisdom. The more we listen, the more human we become. The more we listen, the more spiritual we become. We are able to rise above ourselves and get in touch with others and with God.

Prayer is about listening: listening to what is in my heart; listening to what others are saying and placing all of this in the hands of a listening God. Prayer is the belief that there exists a caring, loving, ever-present listening God. In this we are strengthened, consoled, and find peace. Prayer can be healing because in prayer we can let go and get in touch with God, who cares for and loves us no matter what he hears and knows about us.

3.

Conflict

Conflict is not only a part of life, it is necessary. One of the major misperceptions about marital breakup is that conflict is the cause of most marital distress or of an eventual divorce. On the contrary, the great majority of marital relationships that are coming apart do so due to lack of or the avoidance of conflict to reach a resolution of a conflict. Part of the art of communicating is being able to engage in appropriate conflict, and this, and conflict resolution, are vitally important ingredients of sound relationships.

Conflict is necessary if a healthy, functioning relationship is to be maintained. When Jesus came into the world, he fell into conflict with that world. Jesus said enigmatically, "I did not come to bring peace, but dissension" (Luke 12:51). Jesus was, at various times, in open conflict with his disciples, the people at large, his own family, and, most frequently, the scribes and Pharisees. The Bible is full of conflict! The psalms reflect the conflict going on within us, among people and between us and God. Any time people attempt to become close to one another, there will be both warmth and friction. In a close relationship, warmth and friction go together. If a relationship becomes stuck, there is neither warmth nor friction. The relationship breaks down. The one important element necessary for keeping a mechanism operating is the lubricant. It prevents burnout or the gears from becoming locked. The necessary lubricant in any close relationship, especially in marriage and families, is appropriate conflict.

As I wrote in *Healing Wounded Emotions*, we have been programmed to view anger as a vice rather than a virtue. Anger is a normal, healthy emotion and needs to be expressed in an appropriate way. We need to distinguish between appropriate anger and inappropriate anger, which can be destructive. We need to realize there is a difference between conflict and violence. Violence is conflict out of control.

When spouses suppress their anger, hurts, or disappointments with one another, and let them build up, it will have a deleterious effect on the relationship. This repressive type of relationship is like a cancer eating away at and eroding the bond of trust between the two people. The partners drift apart emotionally, at first unknowingly. Gradually, they realize they are emotionally distant from each other and become sexually uninterested. They panic. They begin to think they no longer love one another and that their marriage is over.

This is not necessarily true. This numb state, in which there are no feelings, is a sign that the relationship is in trouble. The parties are stuck. Underneath the numbness are hidden layers of hurt, anger, even hate and rage. The partners need to start surfacing all the accumulated, unresolved debris within themselves. They need to begin a serious, difficult dialogue. One of the painful aspects of such communication is that disturbing misinterpretations, unresolved differences, long-time resentments, and deep wounds will be exposed.

With regard to extramarital affairs, they are destructive and unfair ways of resolving obvious and/or usually unrecognized discontent in the marriage. Partners are often attempting to have their unmet emotional and sexual needs met in the affair. Such liaisons almost never become permanent and viable relationships. Sometimes they are stepping stones out of a marriage. Affairs are symptomatic of a problematic marriage. They always indicate repressed or suppressed anger at the other spouse, as well as other underlying, unresolved conflicts in the marriage. Silenced conflicts are deadly. Healthy conflicts can be the saving grace by which God's healing power can work.

Repressed conflict can manifest itself in all types of physical problems and emotional difficulties, such as anxiety, depression, cold silence, sexual distancing, and passive-aggressive behavior, to mention only a few. The relationship goes flat, it's without passion and intimacy, while spiritually it lacks meaning and inspiration.

Many people decide prematurely that their marital relationship is over. They decide to separate or to seek out other distractions—like having an affair, or becoming immersed in outside activities or interests. Or they may maintain a tolerant relationship without dealing with underlying tension. Many people divorce prematurely before giving themselves a chance to address underlying issues in their relationship. In so doing, they never allow themselves the opportunity to genuinely encounter each other.

It's true, direct and honest communication may lead to anger and conflict. God knows nobody wants conflict. There are two large, but invisible, signs hanging over the doorways of most American homes. The signs read: "Peace At Any Price" and "Don't Rock the Boat."

Sometimes the unresolved, buried hurts and anger that exist in a relationship eventually emerge in disastrous explosions or other forms of emotional overreaction. This type of conflict is destructive. People say vicious things to one another that they don't necessarily mean, and much unnecessary hurt is the result. The parties are out of control. After an explosion, they are regretful and ashamed of their behavior, but they once again bury their hurt and anger until the next build-up takes place and the next explosion occurs. This cyclical pattern of destructive conflict can be changed only when the partners are involved in learning how to deal with their hurts, angers, and disappointments openly and promptly on a regular basis. However, if the partners fear conflict, they tend to avoid these necessary disagreements, thus setting themselves up for unhealthy periodic explosions.

When we allow people to treat us miserably or abusively without being assertive because we fear conflict, we eventually lose respect for ourselves. Those who mistreat us have no respect for us because we take such abuse and they will continue to treat us harshly.

Some small conflicts we may choose to avoid because the person is not that important to us, or the issues are too inane and are not worth emotional energy being expended to deal with them. However, some of us have the tendency to avoid, minimize, and rationalize too many of our conflicts under the guise that they are insignificant issues when really fear is the underlying motivation. If so, we need to be more honest with ourselves. Talking such issues over with a trusted friend who can help us to be more honest with ourselves would be helpful.

Not all conflicts bring about a resolution of problems. In fact, the problem may even worsen in some situations. At least we have the satisfaction that we faced the conflict and did the best we could. The rest we place in God's hands. Sometimes people live in such conflictual atmospheres that they need to pick and choose their battles and prioritize which issues are worth fighting about or else they would be in continual conflict.

Those couples who are constantly in conflict live in a hostile, aggressive atmosphere featuring blaming, personal attacks, emotional or even physical abuse. These people need to learn how to fight fairly and to find a resolution of their ongoing and never-ending conflicts that may have become a way of life. Such people would probably benefit from joining an anger-management training group.

The kinds of conflict I have just described are not the types of conflict that are to be condoned or encouraged. However, these kinds of destructive conflicts are what most people understand by conflict. What we have been taught or learned about conflict has been negative: don't do it; it's a sin; it's dangerous; it can lead to rejection; conflict implies violence, blaming, someone's having to be right or wrong; it's a power struggle. No wonder we fear conflict

We need to own our conflicts and take responsibility for them.

and avoid it. The type of conflict I'm encouraging and that's necessary is the conflict that normally arises when two or more people are living together in an atmosphere of honesty. In such an atmosphere, where people are open and honest with one another, there will be disagreements, differences, and painful revelations. This is normal and inevitable, otherwise a relationship is superficial and, possibly, dishonest. In seeking honest relationships conflict is a real possibility.

CONFLICT IS INEVITABLE

Let's discuss the sort of appropriate conflict that occurs in healthy relationships, conflict that is inevitable and which can be a source of growth. Conflict can help keep a relationship in good shape by forcing people to process their healthy differences, disagreements, and misinterpretations. Conflict is a creative aspect of any relationship. In the book of Genesis, God created an orderly universe out of a mass of confusion, the sort of confusion that often accompanies conflict. Conflict offers us opportunities to bring about changes in our relationships. That's why we see conflict as an opportunity for growth.

What can we learn about conflict that is positive? First, it's a challenge. It happens inevitably when people live together, and in all close relationships. Conflict surfaces new information and indicates that something needs to be addressed or resolved. In conflict, we gather an abundance of information that we have not known about the other person; unanswered needs and unrecognized feelings, misperceptions and disagreements can be clarified and brought into the open. We begin to realize that change, adjustments, and compromises need to be made. We become more sensitive to one another. At times, we will be shocked and overwhelmed by the revelations that conflict surfaces. But differences in people are not bad—they are normal. Conflict will bring them to light.

We need to own our conflicts and take responsibility for them. We need to dispel the negative tapes about conflict that originated in our childhood, dispel the concept of winning and losing, of blaming, or of assuming that there's something wrong with one or the other. Often we may have to take the initiative to address a conflict. We are not bad persons for starting a conflict but courageous and seeking the truth that sets us free.

Indeed conflict helps us maintain our identity so we don't become swallowed up or controlled by another person. We also recognize and establish boundaries with each other. Control and submission are destructive of a healthy relationship. It is in the area of differences that a marriage either grows, stagnates, or dies. This is the stage at which people divorce prematurely before they have allowed themselves the opportunity to understand and resolve their differences. Rather than seeing themselves as incompatible, wouldn't it be better if they saw themselves as different but equal?

Healthy conflict teaches us to negotiate with one another. This is based on the theory that roles, whether in an intimate relationship or a working relationship, emerge from a process. People need to talk-out the issues and listen to one another as they share their thoughts and feelings, their opinions and viewpoints, without becoming defensive with each other.

Spouses come from different backgrounds, with different views on areas such as how to handle money, raise children, where and how to celebrate holidays, whether the mother should work, and so on. Spouses learn to share information and to negotiate with that new information in mind. They learn to agree on some matters, to cooperate, to compromise, and to tolerate one another's quirks. All this brings about a better understanding and helps people develop trust in one another. The spouses not only come to know each other more intimately, they get to know themselves better because of their interaction. Knowing one another deeply is a significant aspect of the spirituality of marriage.

If we behave this way in all our relationships, we can also clarify for ourselves what we think, what we perceive, how we feel, and what our needs are. Such behavior dispels tension, confusion, and misinterpretations. We can make the necessary adjustments for dealing with another and we can better know each other's needs. When all this happens we feel relieved and better about ourselves and each other. It's like the calm after a storm.

Conflict also helps us overcome rigidity and become more flexible with one another. That's why when one spouse always gives in to the other for the sake of peace, that spouse is not only relinquishing his or her own identity and self-respect, but enabling the other person to become more rigid and more controlling. This is a deleterious pattern found in some marriages.

When we have a gut feeling that something is not right in a relationship—anxieties are building, resentments mounting, or we are beginning to become irritated over insignificant issues—we need to ask what is bothering us, and then begin to communicate with the other about it.

When we hesitate to communicate and neglect to heed warning signs, we are asking for trouble. Sometimes we say we don't want to get the other person upset or we are afraid of hurting their feelings. But this is merely making excuses. We are afraid of conflict. We are "in denial" and indulging in rationalization. If we can recognize the fear of conflict that we all have, we can be a greater support to one another as we try to face unpleasant issues. We break down the walls of resistance to conflict when we share our anxieties about conflict.

The fear of hurting another as a reason for avoiding conflict is one of the most common excuses I hear. But this is a cop-out. We often mask this fear of conflict under the guise that it is unchristian to hurt another's feelings. To think this way is to misunderstand an important religious teaching. Sometimes we fear rejection, being hurt ourselves, or not being liked, or of losing control of ourselves, or even of violence.

Can anyone in a healthy, honest relationship avoid the normal hurt that occurs when we have to be painfully truthful with one another? This hurt goes with the territory. Hurting another's feelings is not a sin! In fact, such honesty can be an act of concern and love for the person. What we need to avoid is speaking the painful truth with malicious words and name-calling. Then the person on the receiving end hears only the vicious language and misses the message being conveyed.

Jesus often hurt people's feelings by being honest, but he also told us directly "The truth will set us free" (John 8:32). He didn't say the truth wouldn't hurt. Indeed, speaking the truth is difficult, but the alternative is much more disastrous to our-selves and our relationships. As Paul writes, "Speak the truth to one another in love" (Ephesians 4:15)—without sarcasm, or rage, or out of a desire to score debating points. Failing to speak honestly is not only detrimental to the other person, but it is a sin of omission. Often there are missed opportunities when possible change, growth, and insights would have occurred among the people concerned.

Hurting another's feelings is not a sin.

Conflict can also indicate a need for change, readjustment, and even role changes in a family. A wife may need her husband to share the housework because she's also working outside the home. When her needs are not being met, or if her partner is especially insensi-tive to her emotional needs, conflict will expose all this and adjust-ments can be made. If, on the other hand, the partners revert to silence rather than engaging in conflict, we can understand why more marriages are dying from silence than violence. Many emo-tional illnesses, like depression, and many physical complaints are often symptomatic of the repression of feelings, especially anger, frustration, or disappointment, and of the avoidance of conflict.

Conflict is inevitable, but it can be positive and creative. It can be structured, when one makes a decision to speak to another and then sets a mutually convenient time and place for the talk. The question is whether we choose to "fight" fairly or unfairly. Reverting to old negative patterns of conflict will not work. Yelling and screaming, overreacting or being aggressive only mean no one's listening. Name-calling, casting aspersions on parents, attempts to shame by making odious comparisons, personal attacks, blaming, unreason-able exaggerations—all these behaviors move people away from the issues at hand and cause them to waste time defending their charac-ters or addressing secondary issues, while avoiding the real prob-lems. Removing oneself from the presence of the other by walking away, changing the subject, introducing other complaints, going into unresolved past issues, using sweeping words like "always" and "never," are all devious ways of sabotaging any constructive conflict. But bringing about constructive conflict is worth the risk of sometimes fighting unfairly. Fighting fairly requires a certain amount of self-control and self-discipline.

Becoming defensive is another way of vitiating the benefits of constructive conflict. When we become defensive, we are not sensitive to what the other person is saying or feeling. We feel as though we are being attacked—so we attack and/or deny. Down deep our defensiveness means: I'm afraid she'll leave me; I'll be abandoned; I don't want to be hurt; he won't love me; something is wrong with me; our marriage is falling apart. When two defensive people meet, the real issue between them is not addressed, and they end up with unproductive conflict that leads to emotional frustration and exhaustion. We can control our defensiveness by holding back from reacting, by becoming calm, and by forcing ourselves to listen intently to the other person. We may want to agree to take time out until we cool off and then return to talk. Thus we not only control our own defensiveness, but are a calming influence on the other as we become more aware of that person.

One of the reasons there are seriously troubled marriages and a high divorce rate is that there are so many issues between the parties concerned that are left unresolved. Some marriages don't have a chance from the start. Some spouses can't resolve conflicts between themselves because they have not addressed the unresolved conflicts within themselves. Such issues as low self-esteem, inadequate feelings about self, shame, and guilt prevent us from engaging in healthy disagreements.

Understanding one another's inner conflicts that are left over from one's family of origin can be beneficial in our conflicts with one another. When I realize that my spouse is still burdened with unresolved issues of anger, hurt, disappointment and abandonment vis-a-vis her parents, then I can avoid taking everything she says personally and understand her better. But she needs to take responsibility to resolve these issues within herself.

Marriage requires people who are secure in themselves and who love themselves in order that they may be able to love and tolerate one another and also have the courage to enter into fairly conducted conflict. Marriage challenges people to mature and grow as individuals. A mature spouse is sensitive and responsive to the other spouse's feelings, issues, and anxieties, but not overwhelmed and infected by them, or else both partners become part of the problem rather than part of the solution. When this happens this is known as co-dependency.

There are certain learnable skills involved in this matter of conflict, such as skills in timing, that is, knowing when and when not to fight, or, if the conflict is dragging on or is out of control, when to call time-out. It might mean scheduling a time to communicate about sensitive issues. These and many other skills can be learned. There is excellent material on this subject available today, such as Deborah Tannen's book *You Just Don't Understand*. There are also seminars that teach the art of conflict resolution and how to fight fairly. We should be teaching this and much more about relationships to everyone in our high schools and colleges. We need to absorb the effective information of experts such as Dr. Phil McGraw, in his book *Relationship Rescue*.

As I have reiterated in these pages we must have some insight and understanding about our family of origin. That family is a veritable treasure chest of information. We go back to it to understand, not to lay blame. From our family we can understand our attitudes toward conflict, how we learned to fight fairly or unfairly, or how we learned not to fight and to hide problems and feelings. Did we ever witness our parents in conflict? Was silence used as a lethal weapon or as a means of avoidance—or both? I have heard many adults say they never saw their parents having any disagreements. What does that say? Did they stuff out of sight what was bothering them? Did they maintain peace at any price? If they fought, how were anger and conflict handled? Were we, as children, punished when we expressed anger or engaged in conflict? Did our parents distinguish between appropriate and inappropriate anger and conflicts?

All these leftovers from our family of origin have sometimes been reinforced by negative religious attitudes that tell us that conflict is a sin to be avoided. We wrongly interpreted the anger and conflict we read of in Scripture. Many people grew up with the three "Ss." Conflict was a sin, so if I got caught up in conflict I felt guilty. Second, conflict made me feel shameful because I was criticized for indulging in it, which made me feel bad about myself, and guilty because "they" told me that fighting was wrong. Finally, conflict causes some suffering so I avoid it.

Some people grew up in extremely conflictual families where they were terribly scarred. Then they either relived their past by living in conflictual marriages or they went to the opposite extreme by making a contract with themselves to avoid all conflict in their marriages. In either case they are being controlled by their past.

What is necessary is a compromise. Accept that part of living involves conflict, but observe the rules of fairness when conflict occurs. We can relive the past by either repeating it, or rebelling against it, or by reconstructing it. We can reconstruct the past by learning from the weaknesses and dysfunction of our family of origin. Then we can construct fair and appropriate ways of expressing conflict and anger, which in time will establish for us healthy, functional relationships.

Some suggestions about fair conflict are:
- Listen intently to the other person;
- Ask for clarification of what the person is saying, thinking, feeling, perceiving, needing;
- Be respectful;
- Disagree without being disagreeable;
- No name-calling or abusive, sarcastic language;
- Avoid interrupting;
- Lessen the emotionality;
- Avoid using "always" or "never" statements;
- Use "I" statements instead of "you" statements;
- Call for a time-out if the conflict is getting out of control, but set up a time to return to the conflict.

All these approaches are not easy, but they can be a tremendous help.

Conflict Is Necessary

It is difficult to conceive that in any area of life where people are gathered together and interacting that conflict will not occur. Conflict is absolutely necessary in order that people can establish boundaries, maintain their identities, know one another, clarify perceptions and issues, resolve problems, and be able to move on with their lives. Conflict breaks down the walls separating us, dislodges the log-jams that keep us stuck, and opens the avenues of communication. In such an atmosphere marriages and families can flourish and grow together in trust and love.

Conflict is a means of growth.

Conflict has always been a characteristic of our Christian heritage. Jesus was in conflict with the religious leaders of his time, the early Christian communities were at odds, Peter and Paul had disagreements, and the conflicts in the Christian communities continue until today. "Where two or three are gathered together in my name there I am in their midst" (Matthew 18:20). And he could have added, "there will be conflict." "Gathered together" doesn't only mean that people agree, but that they disagree.

Learning how to be in healthy conflict forces us to confront the negative tapes that are inside ourselves. These form our conflicts with ourselves. Our relationship with ourselves is the most important relationship we have. If we think and feel badly about ourselves, we will collapse when we find ourselves in the simplest of conflicts with another person. So we need to affirm who we are, to love and forgive ourselves, and to take the anger we feel at ourselves and use it creatively to bring about change within ourselves. When we do let someone get to us and make us feel worthless, we need to be compassionate with ourselves and take responsibility for allowing the other person to make us feel guilty or ashamed, or to overreact. I need to focus on myself and realize I'm the only person that I can change and that when I have a handle on myself, I can make changes and exert control over myself.

Certain people, because they suffer from a severe pathology like a deep mistrust, or hate, paranoia, or schizophrenia, are not good candidates for creative, healthy conflict. Likewise people who are prone to violence or rage. They will have to be avoided or dealt with by group intervention, or in other appropriate and protective ways. Their contact with reality is very poor and distorted, and they cannot achieve any insight into themselves. They lack control of themselves. We need to be lovingly firm with them.

Of course, it goes without saying that, if conflict with a dangerous person could be harmful to myself, I need to avoid such an encounter by perhaps distancing myself physically and emotionally from that person. An estranged wife dealing with a husband who has been violent will need another person present for her protection when he comes to pick up the children.

It is essential that we teach our children from their earliest years that conflict is normal, necessary, and inevitable. We need to teach them the difference between fair and unfair conflict. We will make sure they know how to "fight," but we won't stop them from reasonable conflict or disagreement among themselves. We will teach them that violence, and physical and emotional abuse are not allowed. What is required is listening to the other and being open and honest. Above all, parents must be models to their children of how to fight fairly. Children can get to know that parents do disagree, do have fights, but go on living, loving, and forgiving each other.

Conflict keeps the painful realities of life before us, but it is in facing these painful realities that we remain emotionally, mentally, and spiritually sound. Relating to one another closely means there will be warmth and tenderness, but also, at times, friction and disagreement.

In summary, conflict in relationships is not only necessary but inevitable. It can provide an opportunity for growth. We gain insight into ourselves, others, and the issues in question. We need to move from negative attitudes about conflict to positive ones. With such a perception of conflict, we will have the capacity not only to maintain our relationships, but to develop them and to nurture the intimacy that we seek and need.

If we are open to life and love, we need to be open to conflict. No one feels comfortable with conflict, but we can't allow the fear of conflict to control our relationships. After we face conflict and go through it we'll feel more at peace and, at the very least, a sense of satisfaction. Conflict is a means of growth because it strengthens our self-confidence. Healthy and fair conflict is a unique part of spirituality because it forces us to walk through painful situations, hopefully transcending them and being transformed by them. We need to allow conflict to have an honored place in our relationships.

4.

Intimacy

Intimacy. People use the word indiscriminately. What is it? How is it attained?

According to a theory developed by Robert Steinberg (1986), love has three distinctive components: passion, an intense desire for another person; intimacy, the sharing of all one's feelings, thoughts, needs, and actions with another; and commitment, the willingness to stay with a person in good times as well as bad. These same ideas about love are verified by Christ's teaching. Regarding passion, Jesus said, "Remain in me, as I remain in you" (John 15:4); intimacy, "I no longer call you servants, but friends because I have shared with you all that the Father has made known to me" (John 15:15); commitment, "Greater love than this no one has than to lay down his life for his friends" (John 15:13).

Intimacy refers to that deep yearning within all of us.

Some people think of sex when they hear the word intimacy, but this is only one small aspect of intimacy. Genuine intimacy also has emotional and psychological components. This is the type of intimacy we are all called to attain. It involves the ability to share mutually and deeply of ourselves with another person.

Sexual sharing flows out of emotional and psychological intimacy. The sexual component can nurture, support, and enhance genuine intimacy, but of itself it is not intimacy. Intimacy refers to that deep yearning within all of us to be connected closely with someone else. Ultimately, that someone is God. Scripture is full of expressions of this yearning, such as Psalm 42: "As the deer yearns for the running water, so my soul yearns for you, O Lord, my God." In Isaiah we read of the intimate relationship between child and mother: "Can a mother abandon her child, and, even if she does, I will never abandon you" (Isaiah 49:15).

This yearning is woven within the very fabric of our being and is the root of spiritual intimacy with God. Many people are unable to identify this yearning or due to serious emotional damage, the yearning is confused and distorted. Nonetheless, it is present in all of us. How we seek to fulfill it is a lifetime task. We can choose constructive and creative means to do this, or destructive means. Even in extreme cases of addiction the goal is ultimately a person's search for intimacy.

Men have been socialized to be emotionally distant. Usually their own father is behind this. In some male institutions men have not been taught how to feel or to be close to anyone. Men are supposed to reason, not feel. We men were never taught to integrate feelings and thinking, to bring them together into our close relationships. We know how to separate one from the other, which may work to some degree in an office situation or in business, but not in our personal lives and relationships.

The journey to intimacy is littered with successes and failures but it's a journey we need to make. It is a human and spiritual quest. If

I am in touch and connected emotionally with myself and have experienced emotional connectedness and closeness with others, I'll be able to experience emotional closeness and connectedness with God.

INTIMACY WITH SELF

How do we begin to attain this intimacy? Intimacy begins when we begin to develop a deep sense of awareness of ourselves, and then a deep sense of awareness of other persons. What is necessary first and foremost is that we attain intimacy with ourselves. Being aware of ourselves means being in touch with our inner world—our thoughts, attitudes, opinions, especially our needs and feelings; even our anxieties and uncertainties, and perhaps, feelings of depression.

We are not always in touch with out inner world or conscious of what is going on inside us, but that level of awareness is not always necessary. Much of our daily lives moves along routinely; but when all of life is lived this way and we neglect to take time to reflect on what's going on in our lives, we are out of touch with ourselves.

Being in touch, being reflective about our thoughts and feelings at certain moments in the day, is necessary if we are to find meaning and integration in our lives. We need to make a concerted effort to take time out each day for ourselves to reflect not only on what has happened, but on how we felt and thought about what happened and how we perceived the world around me during this or that experience. It could be a tragic event in the news, or the sudden illness of a dear friend, or hurt feelings caused by a rude remark. I often suggest that people take a reflective, prayerful time-out at the end of the day to process what has happened to them during that day.

It is amazing how many unprocessed experiences we carry around within us. No wonder we become bogged down and just plain unsure of what we think and feel on so many issues. We're out of touch with our hurts, our shocks, our disappointments, our losses. We're even unaware of the joys, surprises, and happy, contented moments of life. The result is that one day flows into another until we can have a lifetime that has been unprocessed, unreflected on, and sometimes, repressed.

As we get in touch with ourselves, we develop insight, which is an understanding of what we think and how we feel and why we behave in such a way. When we gain insight into ourselves we are experiencing the Holy Spirit at work in us, but God works in us only if we work along with him. When we are reflective, God sheds light on our lives. It is within this context that we begin to understand some of the questions we have about ourselves.

With new-found insights about ourselves, we are able to move on to the next stage, which is more difficult and which I call integration. This means being able to bring together our life's experiences and, as a result, to bring about change in our lives, which, we may come to realize, has often been controlled by past experiences. All this then leads to an intimacy and closeness with ourselves. It leads to finding a wholeness, to knowing more about ourselves, to becoming comfortable with ourselves and with what we think and feel. It means coming to some sort of understanding and acceptance of ourselves and of our past.

The first and most important relationship we have is the one with ourselves. If we are not comfortable with ourselves, in touch with ourselves, if we don't know ourselves, how can we attain a level of intimacy with another? In our relationships with others we can learn much about ourselves, if we can focus on the feelings and thoughts occurring within us as we interact with others.

INTIMACY WITH ANOTHER

Becoming intimate with another person means being in touch with that person's inner world. This means knowing what she thinks, what she perceives, what she needs, and, above all, what she feels. There has to be a mutual sharing about this. This type of open and honest disclosure will bring about a deeper level of trust in a relationship. Such intimacy can develop only over a period of time. It will require hard work. There are no quick ways to attain it. Time and risk-taking are necessary. Failures, disappointments, hurts, anger, confusion, and conflict will be experienced.

Becoming emotionally close to another is painful at times, and we have to be able to sustain a certain amount of vulnerability. Gradually, as we become more mutually open and honest in our self-disclosure to one another we will deepen our trust in each other.

Trust is a major ingredient in developing intimacy. It is the foundation upon which a loving relationship is founded.

To be intimate with another we need to share with that other our brokenness, our disappointments, and our frustrations, as well as our joys and satisfactions. For intimacy to happen we need to articulate to one another how we think and feel about our own lived experiences and about what we are experiencing together. That means that we need to talk regularly about what's happening to us and how we feel about what's going on between us (or what isn't going on), and about how we feel about it all.

Do we unthinkably let one day just flow into another? If so, eventually an emotional log-jam will build up within us, a log-jam made up of an accumulation of unspoken and unresolved experiences. This is the predicament in which so many married couples find themselves. If this happens, the achievement of intimacy will be blocked. Think of the frustration felt by so many wives who ask their husbands when they return from work: "What happened today?" only to receive the same answer each day: "Nothing." Responses like that prevent people from sharing their lived experiences. On the other hand, these seemingly unimportant moments present golden opportunities for our getting to know one another and for entering another's world.

Open and honest communication, including attentive listening, is the skill by which we become sensitized to one another. Insensitivity to one another in our relationships, especially in marriage and family, prevents intimacy from becoming a reality.

Sometimes the fear of failure or the memory of past failures in relationships haunts us. We are not sure we want to be known and we fear we will not be accepted or understood. Maybe we'll be hurt, or not liked, or found wanting, or not heard, or rejected. If this is what our past experience has been or if similar memories from our family of origin bedevil us, then we will fear to risk making any attempt to develop an intimate relationship.

It's not surprising that people sabotage possible intimate relationships. Unless we are willing to face the pain that goes with achieving intimacy, deal with our failures, and take the risks involved, we will not be able to experience the fruits of intimacy. That's why so much premature sexual activity goes awry. It is an attempt to find intimacy, but it is a shortcut, one that circumvents the pain of becoming firmly rooted in the life of another person.

INTIMACY AND FAMILY OF ORIGIN

Much of our understanding of intimacy depends on what we experienced in our family of origin. Did the members of my family feel a sense of emotional closeness with one another? Were we emotionally expressive with one another in the family? Did we deeply share the joys and sorrows of our lives? Were our parents emotionally expressive with one another in words and deeds? Did we live in a trusting atmosphere in which we were able to talk freely and openly, express our feelings, our anger, our affection? Or did we feel uncomfortable expressing emotion, to the point where we kept our feelings to ourselves. Intimacy involves that open and honest dichotomy: "I love you and I hate you, I agree with you and I disagree with you, I'm pleased and displeased with you—but I am with you." Many on the journey to intimacy want to deal only with warm feelings and to avoid the difficult feelings, disagreements, and differences. Such a journey will lead nowhere.

If our family did not provide us with the skills for developing intimacy, then we need to realize that we need to develop these skills in our own lives—and it can be done! If our families are severely damaged in these areas I have mentioned we need to recognize that damage, feel the attendant pain, deal with it, reveal it, and then be healed of it before moving on. We need to process and work through the past. As John Bradshaw said so well: "We can't put the past in the past until we pass through it."

No one has a perfect family background. All families lack something. We all come from some lesser or greater degree of dysfunction. Yet the reality is that things can be different if we are willing to change and move on. We need the courage to return to our past, to acknowledge the painful truths there, the neglect, the hurt, the damage, and to start dealing with it by talking about it. We need to have friends with whom we can share such delicate and sensitive material. We need support groups or good counseling. We go back to the past to understand, not blame. When we understand the past we are able to heal, to let go, to forgive, and to move on.

People in a close relationship need to share their family of origin experiences with each other. Sharing the good and the bad is part of their being intimate with one another. In this mutual exchange, which can be both painful and interesting, both enlightening and enjoyable, the couple come to a deeper understanding of each other and of themselves.

We go to the past to understand, not blame.

There is a pre-marriage program called "When Families Marry." It couldn't be more on target because when two people marry, they carry into the marriage their own family treasures but also much unresolved baggage that needs to be recognized and addressed. Most young couples need to recognize how they related to, interacted with, communicated with, and treated others in their families because the only model for marriage and family each one of them has is their own. The characteristics, good and bad, of the family of origin are brought to the marriage.

Most of the time, when marriage counselors are dealing with marital problems they are really dealing with unresolved issues connected with families of origin. Perhaps the young man never saw his parents fight, but also never saw them show any loving and tender emotions toward one another. The young man sees marriage as a male-dominated relationship, as was his father's relationship with his mother. A girl who never experienced emotional closeness with her father wonders about her acceptance by males. The young woman who believes in being a wife and mother ignores her own needs and desires as she caters to her children and her husband—as her mother did. All those who never witnessed their parents being angry with one another, or who saw their parents being full of rage or acting violently toward one another, will be affected by this parental behavior.

Similarly, men and women who came from alcoholic or severely dysfunctional families may be full of guilt, repressed, angry, or co-dependent. It is not that these people cannot develop healthy, intimate relationships; but they will not be able to form intimate relationships until they deal with the unresolved family issues. Unless people receive proper information and understanding about their background and about the true meaning of intimacy, dysfunctional behavior will continue to perpetuate itself. Unhealthy patterns of relating are passed on from generation to generation.

A realistic view of what commitment is about in a relationship, especially in a marriage, implies that the spouses agree to work together on the personality problems and differences of belief and behavior they recognize in each other, and which stem from each other's pasts. Such a commitment is not only realistic but creative because out of all these painful issues, a new relationship can emerge through cooperation, collaboration, and conflict.

WHY "GOOD" MARRIAGES FAIL

Why do seemingly "good" marriages fail after many years? One reason is that although the spouses shared the raising of their children, the managing of their finances, and the other aspects and problems involved in being a family, they never shared themselves with each other. They never developed an emotional, psychological bond. When the children have established themselves on their own, outside the home, spouses realize they don't know each other and are emotionally distant from each other. Something is missing in their relationship. It is always painful to witness lengthy marriages devoid of vitality, just when the spouses could be enjoying this time of their lives and celebrating a new era. Today people in marriages of twenty-five years or more are increasingly finding their way to counseling or the divorce court. They lost themselves in many things but not in each other.

The most important relationship in a family is always the relationship between husband and wife. We don't necessarily always acknowledge that; but as that relationship goes, so goes the family. Children know they are loved and feel secure when they realize that their parents love one another. Therein lies the disaster of divorce and how it significantly affects children. That lingering doubt persists in children. "If Mom and Dad don't love each other, how do I know if they love me, even when they assure me they do?"

Researchers today offer much data showing the damage divorce does to children. The children can be helped to heal, but the parents also need to heal, and both parents and children need psychological and spiritual help. The only model children have of marriage is the model they see their parents living out. If that relationship lacks intimacy, what do the children bring to their own marital relationships in the area of intimacy and communication? Even sophisticated and well-educated people are no better at living a healthy married life than their parents were.

Our children today, in spite of all their education and sophistication, are marrying as their parents did and bringing to marriage the same hang-ups. These children needed to witness a mother and father who not only loved but who showed affection, who expressed anger and engaged in conflict with one another, parents who deeply shared their lives together, especially on the emotional level; who walked together through their anxieties, uncertainties; and doubts; who walked through the dark valleys and danced on the mountaintops; who struggled with their differences and then went on living together, able to let go when that was called for, and to move on together. That's a realistic view of what marriage is about: a commitment that reflects a deep intimacy.

The most important relationship in a family is between husband and wife.

It's good to remember that our parents, in trying to raise us, did the best they knew how. They didn't have the kind of information I'm sharing with you. But we need to recognize and understand their shortcomings and how we were perhaps damaged and neglected so we can change and move on. Remember, we go back to understand, not to blame. If we get stuck in blaming, we'll never move on.

Remaining stuck can become a comfortable way to hide, or it can be a form of resistance to moving on. In other words, we will never experience the peace, joy, hope, and happiness of the kingdom within ourselves if we don't look forward. If the most important relationship in the family is between husband and wife, then that relationship needs to be continually nurtured despite the presence of children—indeed such nurturing benefits the children.

Researchers who have been studying marital breakdown notice the stress on the husband-wife relationship that the birth of the first child brings with it. In *USA Today*, July 8, 2004, John Gottman, professor emeritus of psychology at the University of Washington, says that many new mothers and fathers experience postpartum depression, increased irritability, a tendency to fight, and a lack of sexual intimacy that can lead to infidelity. Writes Gottman: "It is a very child-centered period when the spousal relationship can get neglected."

My own experience with couples is that over the years, as the size of family increases, wives and husbands must be reminded to make a concerted effort to take time to nurture their own relationship. So many times I've heard middle-aged spouses sadly bemoan the fact that, after the children were grown, they, the parents, had to admit they had neglected their own relationship. So often I have had to challenge younger couples to come up with a game plan to schedule time for themselves away from the children. It is not always easy to make this time, but it is necessary for the survival of the marriage.

Sexual Intimacy

I mentioned previously that sexual intimacy appropriately flows out of established emotional and psychological intimacy. Sexual intimacy must celebrate an emotional intimacy that has been experienced previously if it is to have any meaning. However, today, sexual relations are not always like that. We may call it sex, sexual intercourse, or relating sexually—but it has nothing to do with sexual intimacy. The result is that more and more people are disillusioned about their relationships, which begin with passionate sex before any deep emotional sharing has been achieved.

People have said to me that if they had to do it over they would make sure they had more sexual experience before getting married. They are referring to the sexual problems they have in their marriage. But the solution isn't more sexual experience. A lack of emotional and psychological intimacy is creating these problems. Lack of awareness of this fact is common throughout our society, among the educated and uneducated, rich and poor, young and old. Erroneous thinking has rationalized sexual behavior with terms such as "casual" or "recreational" sex in which "no one gets hurt." The trouble with all this is not so much sexual as it is destructive of the person's ability to deeply and emotionally relate to another person. What is being destroyed in these people is the ability to be intimate, to relate genuinely. Becoming prematurely sexually involved in a relationship often sabotages the possibility of forming a deep emotional, lasting relationship.

Sexual intimacy can enhance and nurture the emotional intimacy that occurs in a trusting relationship. Both forms of intimacy are uniquely interwoven and are sensitive to each other. When emotional intimacy begins to unravel, this will affect the quality and frequency of the sexual relationship. It may even cause the sexual relationship to cease. When married partners are talking with me about their emotional conflicts, it is evident that their sexual relationship is also in trouble even before they openly address that issue. On the other hand couples entering counseling with sexual issues as the presenting problem will eventually have to deal with the real problem: their ailing personal relationship.

People are often searching, through sexual experience, for something missing in their lives. I have heard so many women say that they are engaged in sexual activity with a man with the hope of finding affection, emotional comfort, and closeness. Men, on the other hand, will come alive and give emotional affection in order to obtain sex. Society today gives ample freedom and permission for sexual experiences, but it doesn't give people understanding of the meaning of emotional intimacy or how to obtain it. Intimacy, as psychologist Fran Ferder states, is not about removing our clothes but removing our masks. It is all about self-disclosure, openness, and honesty with another in a close relationship.

We need to help our young people get in touch with that deep yearning for intimacy, which is basically good and God-given but which needs to be explained and developed. They need to understand that the sexual side of themselves involves yearning for emotional closeness. Since this emotional intimacy is something they often have not experienced in their families, they stumble along unknowingly in their search for such intimacy. Then sexual activity becomes as casual and as common as going down to McDonald's for a hamburger. The spirit of genuine intimacy is destroyed, and the capacity for genuine love is being eroded.

One of the things that is not well-known about intimacy is that psychological and emotional intimacy can be complete without any sexual expression. In other words, two persons can share a deep emotional intimacy without having sex. Some may want to call such a relationship platonic, but it is something much deeper than that.

What Intimacy Is and Is Not

It is important to realize what intimacy is not. It does not involve controlling a person or submitting to another person. It's not about power games. It is not dependency or co-dependency; rather, it's about the interdependence of independent people. It is not obsession with or possession of another. It is not addiction to another person or absorption by that person.

People who enjoy intimacy allow one another space. They know there are limits and boundaries in relationships and that one's own identity is not founded on another person. Intimacy is not infatuation or romanticism, although intimacy can be romantic. It is not a state of emotional helplessness, but brings about a deep sense of security and trust regarding the other person, in spite of emotional hurts and disappointments. It is a lifelong quest for all of us who seek it; and, truly, we all need it.

Issues today like promiscuity, premarital sex, divorce, loneliness, living together before marriage, addictions, and many other human problems and questions with which we are struggling are linked together by a deeper common issue: our ability or inability, our willingness or unwillingness to choose intimacy. Thus, the real issue is the attaining of intimacy with self, with another, and with God. But we can't attain what we don't understand, and we can't understand until we are able to identify and interpret that deeper yearning within all of us for intimacy.

5.

The Most Important Relationship

The core of Jesus's teaching is summed up in the verse "Love God, and your neighbor as yourself." This message sets the tone for all Jesus' teaching, which is fundamentally about relationships. It is here that sound psychology and the teaching of Jesus meet, and there is no contradiction between the two. Christians sometimes focus on the love of God and of neighbor, pay less attention to the command of Jesus to love oneself. But according to Scripture, it has equal billing. Actually, the most important relationship we have is our relationship with ourselves. To love oneself is necessary if we wish to love others and God. As this relationship with ourselves goes, so goes our relationship with others—and with God.

If we don't get along with ourselves, if we are not comfortable, with, confident about, and at peace with ourselves, how can we possibly get along with others? When our relationship with the self is out of sync, we lose a sense of balance and boundaries within other relationships. A healthy self-love acts as an inner compass, which keeps us headed on the right course in our relationships.

SELF AND MARITAL DIFFICULTIES

One of the most common, but often unnoticed, causes of marital difficulties is a lack of self-love on the part of one or both of the partners. It requires a certain amount of self-love to sustain and maintain one's stability in the face of anger, disagreement, and dislike stemming from the other spouse. After a divorce, when the dust settles, the lawyers are paid, and if and when the blaming ceases, the divorced person might realize that the marriage failed because "I failed to love myself enough." Likewise, a second marriage will run into great difficulty if the person who has already failed in one marriage has not developed a love of self.

Loving self means knowing and taking responsibility for one's problems—like unresolved conflicts, failure to develop, or a lack of happiness. This is the key to making relationships work. The only person I can ever begin to change is myself, with the possibility that I may then be able to influence another to change. Breaking unhealthy patterns of relating does not mean trying to change or blame another, but rather, using the courage and energy that flows from myself to adjust my own behavior.

Over the years, I have seen relationships, especially in marriage and family, improve because one person was willing to change. Much time and energy are wasted when we attempt to change one another. Why not use our energy to change ourselves instead of attempting to change another? This doesn't mean giving in or losing one's identity or self-respect, but learning to respond and deal with another in a mature and appropriate manner. When we respond reasonably to another person, we are in control of ourselves. When we overreact to another person, we are not in control; in fact, the other is in control. The Serenity Prayer says it well:

Lord grant me the serenity
　to accept the things I cannot change,
　the courage to change the things I can,
　and the wisdom to know the difference.

Herein lies the basis of inner peace and happiness, which arises from contentment and satisfaction with oneself. If we did the best we could in any given situation, then whether we succeed or not, whether the other person responds to us positively or negatively, whether things get better or worse, we will be satisfied with our own behavior and at peace with ourselves. These are the fruits of a loving relationship with self.

Many people don't understand the meaning of healthy self-love. They fear talking about loving themselves because they think others might consider them selfish or self-centered. They feel uncomfortable with the idea of loving oneself. Loving self is sometimes equated with selfishness, self-centeredness, and narcissism. As children, we were taught that it was wrong and even shameful if we spoke affirmingly of ourselves. I can remember being told not to use the pronoun "I" too frequently lest I be considered egotistical.

We need to understand the difference between self-love and selfishness. A person with healthy self-love has a good sense of self, takes care of self in all ways, has self-respect, and takes responsibility for his life, yet is still able to focus on others and connect with them. Love of self means being able to establish a balance and boundaries between self and others, thus fostering individuality and good relationships. When a person is aware of and appreciates his or her individuality, that person has the possibility of successfully relating to another individual and of allowing the other person to be an individual.

A person who is self-centered and selfish does not have a good sense of self; rather, they are obsessed with self and the self's issues. They have difficulty focusing on others or connecting with others. Such a person does not establish boundaries when dealing with others because his or her own vision of self is fixated on his or her own self. Such a person lacks the ability to relate to others because he or she cannot properly see or hear another person.

Before we can practice self-love, we must first accept without reservation that loving ourselves is indeed the most important love relationship we have. Once we believe this, we can be open to developing the skills operative in loving ourselves. Self-love demands hard work, determination, education, truthfulness, and the wisdom that comes from the experience of trial and error. All this connects the concept of self-love with the reality of self-love, the practice of which is an art.

In the following pages, I will expand on these characteristics of a healthy self-love:

it is demanding;

it is difficult;

it requires discipline;

it requires a discovery of our past;

it calls for a dedication of the self to be oneself.

Self-love Is Demanding

Developing a loving relationship with ourselves is demanding. It requires truthfulness, openness, and an honesty about our lives, a willingness to evaluate our perceptions, thoughts, feelings, needs, behaviors, and interactions with others. It requires that we be critical of ourselves without condemning ourselves. It calls us to be the best we can be without our becoming perfectionists. Because I am always with myself, should I not be my own best friend, feel good about myself, and be happy with myself, in spite of the difficulties and the mishaps of life?

Becoming comfortable with myself means that I am in touch with my thoughts and feelings, that I'm learning to be aware of all my feelings without any guilt or shame. Our feelings are indicators of what is going on within; they tell us about ourselves. If I say "I'm angry when people tell ethnic jokes," that can reflect my past hurt over such jokes when they were directed at me. Or it might indicate that I have not accepted my own ethnic origins. Or it might indicate that I am sensitive to the unnecessary hurt that jokes cause others. My feelings give me important information about myself. The more I can be comfortable with such feelings, the better I can manage them and, if necessary, express them appropriately.

Besides accepting my feelings, I need to listen to and respect my needs. Like our feelings, our needs are gifts from God. They are part of our humanness; they are not weaknesses. Recognizing our needs is a part of healthy self-love and has nothing to do with selfishness. In the turmoil of life much unrest occurs because people do not accept their own needs. They either suppress them or act them out in unhealthy ways. If we do not recognize our needs and satisfy them appropriately, our needs will be in control and will be acted out inappropriately.

Loving ourselves is the most important love relationship.

A loving relationship with self demands that we care for ourselves in all ways, physically, emotionally, and spiritually. We need to appreciate the gift of life and who we are. As stated in the Psalm: "Oh Lord, I thank you for the wonderfulness of my being" (Psalm 139:14).

How do we care for our body? Do we wash, eat, drink, and dress properly? Do we avoid what will harm our health? Do we rest and relax? Do we exercise? Visit our doctors when necessary? Follow through with medication and treatment when needed? Do we take care of ourselves intellectually? Do we appreciate education? Seek it as long as we can? Do we read worthwhile material? Do we care for ourselves emotionally?

Many people do not understand themselves or their feelings. They educate the mind, but neglect to care for the emotional dimension of their lives. For the most part, people's problems in life are usually not about intellectual issues, but lie more within the emotional area, within themselves and within relationships. The foundational education we receive about our emotions comes from what we experience in our family of origin. Our parents did the best they knew how, to rear us, but in the area of emotions, they were limited. They did not have available to them the enormous amount of psychological information that we are enriched with today.

These days, with the availability of popularized psychology and self-help books, we are better able to inform ourselves about our emotionality. Counseling has lost the negative stigma often attached to it in the past. People now see it as a positive necessity that anyone can benefit from. The better we know ourselves, the better equipped we are to guide our own lives with more responsibility, and the better we are able to understand others, the more we will be able to train and guide our children as they try to deal with their emotions.

There is no reason for anyone to be living in psychological darkness at this time. Indeed we need to be more interested in ourselves psychologically, and to take more responsibility for ourselves in this area.

LOVING OURSELVES IS DIFFICULT

The test of genuine self-love is the ability to maintain a balance between loving ourselves and loving others. This requires constant vigilance and honesty with others and ourselves. Such love maintains and respects one's own individuality while respecting and allowing the other to be an individual. Secure love of self can stand up confidently for itself while maintaining confidence and trust in another.

In a loving relationship, we share much in common. We agree on many things, and have common goals and values. There will be areas of difference, which are not only normal but healthy. Having a respect for one another's differences is necessary for the maintenance of individuality. We learn to adjust to, adapt to, and compromise with each other. We are secure enough in ourselves to accept the other person as she or he is.

At times, there will be in our relationships some differences that lead to a certain amount of appropriate conflict, anger, disappointment, and hurt. This is inevitable and even necessary, in good, healthy relationships. Arriving at a resolution or compromise over differences strengthens the relationship and makes it more secure. Avoiding conflict and anger is not only dishonest, but harmful to a relationship. Unresolved issues like that always remain just below the surface and will surface in destructive ways.

During times of conflict and differences our self-love is most vulnerable; we can begin to lose confidence in ourselves. This is the critical time when we need to maintain a belief in ourselves, refusing to submit or try to control the other, and trying to work through the conflict. Thus individuality is maintained and the relationship strengthened.

Our self-love is threatened when a conflict leads to inappropriate or emotionally abusive behavior. We may be hurt at times like these, but we cannot allow ourselves to be emotionally destroyed or get pulled into the other person's destructive behavior. When abuse occurs, we may have to remove ourselves from the situation or relationship as a means of self-preservation. These are not easy situations, but the most important principle in any relationship or situation is how I deal with any problematic situation. The focus and responsibility is ultimately on myself, no matter how wrong or unfair the other person may be. I need to face the situation and not get stuck in blaming and/or complaining. I need to respond to the person or the situation in an appropriate manner. I redirect my anger by being assertive, my hurt by being more confident. I do not become passive. I do not overreact. Both of these behaviors are destructive to myself, primarily, but also to the situation.

Love maintains and respects one's own individuality.

When I act constructively like this, I will realize this is the energy that gives me the power to take action for myself. This is confident self-love. No matter what the outcome may be, I have the satisfaction and inner peace of knowing that I responded appropriately. I took responsibility for myself. Maintaining our self-love and self-respect in such difficult situations is the only possible way of improving a relationship. If the relationship worsens, at least our relationship with ourselves is maintained. In the last analysis the individual who behaves constructively will always survive an unhealthy relationship.

So much time and energy are wasted in relationships in which we try to change others. Relationships are not about control, but about mutual interaction as we work through difficult issues and situations. The more we attempt to change another, the more they will resist, which is another form of their own control over us. We allow their resistances to cause us frustration and discouragement, which defeat us. Using our energy to change ourselves will be more profitable and effective in the long run.

The courage to say what I think and feel and to be flexible in how I handle a difficult problem or person means I am witnessing to the truth. Sometimes, others stubbornly resist and become more rebellious when we change. In the long run, however, I will realize that I did what I could do. The issue is not whether the other person listens, agrees, or changes; the primary issue is that I need to say and do what is necessary out of a sense of my own self-respect and dignity. This helps us to be hopeful about our relationships because we are coping, and when we cope, we can hope. Jesus' life reflects this when he dealt with resistant scribes and Pharisees: he spoke out and took a stand, then he let go of trying to reach them but continued to proclaim his message.

Parents who take a stand with difficult and rebellious children need to operate like this. In counseling, I have often experienced the wisdom of the principle: give me the parents and they will heal the children. This involves parents taking control of the situation by being in control of themselves. When parents lose control of their behavior and language they lose control of the children. Then parents lose confidence in themselves and the respect of their children.

When children are in charge and in control of the family, they need to be fired and the parents rehired. Sometimes it means tough love, which requires drastic action. It means parents having enough self-love to take such loving action.

A silent spouse who is "taking" neglect and indifference from the other spouse needs to speak up and be assertive in expressing how hurt and angry she is. She needs to express that she is not deserving of such treatment. Often, this can be the beginning of healthy change in the marital relationship. When a bad situation has been allowed to develop because one spouse has accepted neglect from the other for years, the possible improvement in such a relationship will occur when the neglected spouse takes responsibility for what she has allowed to happen. The other spouse may not listen or change; however, the neglected or abused spouse has changed, has taken a stand and will no longer accept such treatment. Who knows, because of this taking a stand by one partner, the other spouse may be influenced or inspired to change. God works through one spouse to touch the other.

In all our relationships, especially in our close ones, there are normal stresses and tensions that impact our maintenance of a loving relationship with ourselves. But if we can achieve that loving relationship with ourselves, the better and healthier our relationships will be with each other. There'll be two people who are individuals, who can share deeply of themselves, be in touch with each other's inner world, and respect their differences. The couple is together but different. This is the experience of intimacy. Healthy self-love leads to a close relationship with another.

SELF-LOVE REQUIRES DISCIPLINE

Self-discipline means saying yes to life. Saying yes means facing up to all the realities of life because this is where God's will is. Mary said, "Be it done to me according to your word" (Luke 1:38). Jesus said "Your will be done" (Luke 11:2). In both situations, "yes" brought about good results: the Incarnation and redemption. Even though so much of life can be unfair, when we daily say our "yes" to God and allow God to work in our lives, good things can happen.

Saying yes means we are willing to be responsible for and take charge of our lives and our relationships. We say: "I will be able to do today what I have to do, for my own personal good. What I do is not determined by other people, by what they do or don't do, but by what I need to do if I am to be truthful to and respectful of myself. Even though I may not be able to determine whether a given situation is going my way or not, my yes means facing up to whatever may be going on at that moment."

My determination to love, to forgive, to be kind and compassionate, to be affectionate, or to reach out to others in need must be part of my yes to life and relationships. Paul says, "Overcome evil by good" (Romans 12:9). Jesus said, "Love your enemies. Do good to those who hate you. Pray for those who persecute you" (Matthew 5:44). In other words, we are to take charge of who we are and live our lives according to what we believe. The challenge of the Christian life is to be willing to accept responsibility for one's life.

The discipline of self-love also means being ready to say no to what is harmful or destructive; no to attitudes, values, or beliefs that may harm me in any way or make me less of a person. We need to

Forgiving ourselves helps us to get back on track.

say no to relationships that are not life-giving. This requires honesty with myself, and commitment to the "truth that will set me free" from the blindness of illusions or delusions about myself.

Knowing what my limitations and boundaries are is not an admission of weakness but testimony to the strength that comes from knowing myself. It means listening to and trusting my inner self. Sometimes people who have been raised in dysfunctional families are left with severely damaged psyches and cannot get in touch with their inner selves. One of the signs that such people are healed is when they can listen and trust their inner self, their instincts, and their intuitions.

Being able to say yes and no to myself establishes boundaries for myself. Yes, I will go to bed at this time because I have to be up early the next morning for work and I have to be efficient. No, I decline that extra drink since I have to drive home. Maintaining appropriate boundaries for myself as well as with others is part of developing balanced and healthy relationships. Setting appropriate boundaries means, for example, that I don't allow people to speak to me or treat me inappropriately or abusively. I don't allow people to touch me inappropriately or make sexual advances. Even in the closest of relationships we have to set up boundaries with each other.

A common example of crossing boundaries occurs when we take responsibility for others' lives, or for their behavior. Parents sometimes do this with their children. Spouses can do it with their spouses. Sometimes we do this out of a sense of unhealthy guilt or from a false sense of trying to help others; thus we enable another, we become co-dependent. We all experience failures in these areas, but we have to avoid becoming full-fledged addicts when it comes to taking responsibility for other people's lives. We must learn to say no out of love for ourselves and others or else we can become a major part of their problem. We find ourselves trying to protect others, perhaps out of anxiety, when really we are trying to control them or the situation.

Having self-discipline means developing structure and order in our lives. How do we plan our day, and arrange time for work and leisure, for reflection and prayer, for interacting with and relating to others? What are our priorities? People who are disorganized accomplish less and can be frustrated. Those who have good organizational skills will enjoy a strong sense of self-satisfaction and a sense of being in charge of their lives.

DISCOVERING OUR FAMILY OF ORIGIN

We will never come to know ourselves fully until we can understand the history of our own family. How the family influenced me, its patterns of relating, the attitudes, values, and beliefs of the members of my family—all are powerful aspects of our family history. They have a significant impact on who we are, for good or ill.

Good traits need to be embellished and improved upon; bad traits need to be eliminated. We have the right and responsibility to process our personal history, just as we do our secular history. In going back, we will come to realize the origin of our weaknesses and our strengths. In our past there lies a tremendous amount of rich information that is vital to our present well-being and self-understanding.

On this journey we can resolve our hurts, anger, disappointments, and losses, so that we can heal our wounds allowing our intellectual and emotional strengths to develop. But how will we be able to climb the mountain of life effectively if we are carrying unresolved baggage that weighs us down? We'd be like the gifted child who can't perform in school because of his or her emotional problems. We are sabotaging ourselves if we are living out what we have not resolved in our past.

DEDICATION TO SELF

The most important commitment I will ever make in life is the commitment to myself. It's a commitment to become the person God calls me to be. This dedication to be oneself is the foundation of healthy self-love.

One of the most necessary skills I will need to sustain this dedication is the willingness to forgive myself. On our journey we will fail and sin. Forgiving ourselves helps us to get back on track, to learn, to let go, and to move on. Much of counseling is not so much about resolving the problems and issues of life as it is about finding some way of coping with or learning to live with them. In this process, forgiving ourselves is a tremendous help. Genuine self-forgiveness impels us to face the consequences of our misbehavior.

Self-love includes being willing to forgive ourselves and to accept our human frailties. We need to have a means of recovery, which means self-forgiveness, or else we can become "stuck." Self-forgiveness helps us to break loose. It calls us not only to deal with the consequences of our misbehavior, but to repent, and if necessary, to make reparation. We come to know ourselves better as we deal with this process. We learn from our failures. Sometimes, not to forgive ourselves can be a cop-out, a refusal to change because we fear change. It can also involve self-centeredness or self-pity, or wanting to indulge in self-hatred.

If I am dedicated to myself I will forgive myself so I can move on with my life. With this type of self-confidence I am prepared to face anything in life. None of us has all the capabilities and knowledge we need. But if we have a deep abiding belief and confidence in ourselves, we know we can cope with whatever may come our way. We will get up every morning with the courage to say yes to life and face whatever may come our way that day.

There is a communication system going on within us, whether we are aware of it or not. We need to listen to what we are saying to ourselves, i.e., the positive and negative messages we send ourselves. It is estimated that we send about 3,000 messages to ourselves everyday. "I can do this task." "I can't do it." "He likes me." "She doesn't like me." They are based on a negative or positive perception of ourselves. This perception can and will change if we change the communication going on within ourselves. The positive statements that we communicate to ourselves are life-giving, while the negative ones are deadly to our self-confidence, self-image, and self-esteem.

Much of the negative thinking we indulge in eventually becomes negative "tapes" we play to ourselves repeatedly. Sometimes we are so accustomed to them we are not even aware that they are playing. When I confront clients about these negative "tapes", they are not always aware of the amount of negativity that they harbor about themselves. Some of these negative tapes originated a long time ago in our childhood; others came along the way from negative messages we received from family members and others, or messages from friends we interpreted negatively, or from failures or mistakes we allowed to infect us.

The kind of negative self-talk that says "I can't do this," or "I can't do that," or "I'm no good," or "people don't like me," or "I'll never be able to accomplish this task" prevents me from growing. It is self-defeating, and stops any growth or healing. It becomes a way of life. Sometimes people do cop out and opt for such a way of life. They become comfortable with it in a strange way. They choose to live inside their illness. They actually fear taking a risk and moving beyond their negative existence. Negative people are not only toxic, they can drive others crazy. They are extremely difficult to live with and can infect other relationships, especially marriages, families, and communities. As self-confident people, we must not allow them to infect us. When they do, we need to take responsibility for not allowing them to erode our own self-confidence.

Negative persons not only think they are losers but also feel and act like losers. What came first, the negative thinking or the negative feelings? Children, especially infants, who have not developed the capacity to think or reason are nothing more than a bundle of feelings. In fact, a baby is very sensitive to what its mother or father may be feeling, especially if the latter are upset. When children feel insecure and anxious they begin to develop negative feelings within themselves. Eventually, as they begin to develop their thinking capacity, they begin to think negatively of themselves. A child might say: "I feel badly about myself, therefore I must be a bad person." Eventually, a much wider pattern of negative thinking and feeling develops within the child. Life then becomes a negative journey. The child's personality becomes shame-based, and that infects her whole life: her choices, her thinking, her feelings and behavior.

As people struggle to change their negative thinking, they must not allow wounded feelings, especially guilt and shame, to overwhelm and influence them. Sometimes, people's thinking and decisions are determined by their negative feelings. Eliminating this way of thinking requires time and practice. We will often fail, and we will need a lot of self-affirming before we can attain a positive way of thinking. Eventually, after the negative thinking becomes more positive the wounded feelings will heal.

Over the years I have counseled many intelligent clients who have been extremely competent and successful in their professional lives, but in their relationships with themselves, they have been negative and unhappy persons. It's not surprising that, in attempting to form relationships with others, they made poor choices. Their relationships with others were superficial, and sometimes unhealthy because of their negative relationship with themselves. They chose negative partners or destructive ones or persons equally insecure, like themselves. They became people pleasers, submissive, or aquiescent to others in order to find acceptance. We must be convinced that we can change our negative tapes, or our relationships with others will be jeopardized. We need to be persistent in improving our thinking about ourselves.

Communication within ourselves has a powerful effect not only on our self-confidence, but on our self-esteem, self-image, and sense of self-worth. It is in these areas of thoughts and feelings that counseling can bring healing and embellishment to the human spirit.

Self-confidence Is a Skill

Self-confidence is not inherited; it must be developed throughout our lives. We can't allow fears, unhealthy guilt, or shame to control us or cause us to avoid what we need to face. Our failures and fears properly handled can help us to build self-confidence. We can learn from them and grow. We need to develop a positive attitude about ourselves and not be infected by negative thinking coming from within ourselves or from others or from a negative world. Another person or situation may hurt us and shake our self-confidence, but we will never allow them to destroy our self-confidence. Positive statements about ourselves and imagining what we can be and do are essential skills in developing self-confidence.

When we gain insight into ourselves we are responsible for integrating that information into our lives in order to make changes in our thinking, feelings, attitudes, and behavior. For example, once a man realizes that his fear and mistrust of authority figures is rooted in his unresolved feelings about his distant, rigid, and demanding father he is now challenged to make some adjustments to his fear of authority figures. He needs to stop displacing anger on them. He needs to resolve the hurt and anger he feels toward his father, which is still controlling his life. He needs to take responsibility for changing his perception of authority figures, while taking some reasonable risks to trust them and interact a little more confidently with them.

We need a positive attitude about ourselves.

All these dynamics—being in touch with our thoughts and feelings, gaining insight from them, and integrating the new information into our lives—brings us to a closer and more intimate relationship with ourselves. We know more about who we are. We are at a place where we can be compassionate, understanding, forgiving toward, and affirming of ourselves. It's a place where we can be critical of ourselves and not condemn ourselves, a place where we can be in honest and open communication with ourselves and be our own best friend. It is this type of loving relationship with ourselves that prepares us for the difficult work of forming a close relationship with another person.

The inner happiness we all seek is a quality we can only find and develop within ourselves. No one can give it to us. No amount of material or external things can produce it. Happiness is the conviction that I am lovable. It is not something that happens to me when I graduate from college, meet the right person, go on the next vacation, or maybe win the lottery. It means enjoying who I am, where I am, and whatever is going on in my life. It is basically an inner contentment with myself. No one can take it away from me. If I allow someone or something to disrupt my happiness I need to ask why I allowed this to happen to me.

I hope some of the thoughts on self-love shared here may be of benefit in helping the reader to realize not only how important self-love is, but also how complex it can be, how interwoven it is in the process of close, loving relationships; and how there needs to be a delicate balance between self-love and loving another.

6.

Forgiveness & Reconciliation

All emotional, psychological, mental, spiritual, and relationship healing requires us to forgive and be forgiven. The gospel story of the paralytic is an example of how Jesus links emotional, spiritual, and physical healing: "I say to you, your sins are forgiven. Pick up your mat and walk" (Matthew 9:2, 6).

Let's not be naïve about the difficulty of forgiveness. If we want forgiveness to work for us and to be a source of healing, we need to understand how the dynamics of forgiveness work, how they operate in us and among people. Forgiveness is not an automatic, casual, or superficial thing—it requires work, effort, and time. Forgiveness is a process; this is the psychological term we will be using frequently in describing the movements of forgiveness.

The process of forgiveness has three movements: the intellectual (volitional), the emotional, and the spiritual. The volitional aspect involves a choice—a decision, an act of the will—to forgive or be forgiven. The emotional is that part of the process that involves our being in touch with the painful feelings that often accompany the act of forgiving or being forgiven, and working through those feelings. The spiritual refers to the part of the process that enables us to let go of hurt and anger and move on with our lives.

FORGIVING SELF

The most difficult and demanding aspect of forgiveness is forgiving oneself. A major reason why people are slow to reconcile is that they do not forgive themselves. Self-forgiveness is not given serious consideration, and very little is preached or written about it. Actually, it is an essential part of healthy self-love.

Only after I have forgiven myself can I rise up to face life's situations again. Only then can I reach out and forgive, be forgiven, and begin the work of reconciliation with others.

I must make the choice to forgive myself. In the midst of self-hate, anger, and disappointment with myself I must take the first step in the process of forgiveness. It is a pure act of the will, contrary to all the negative feelings I may be experiencing. I want to do it.

In the touching story of the prodigal son, the young man forgave himself first before he made his journey back to the father. In an act of self-love and self-preservation he realized he had to do something to help himself. Inherent within that self-love was self-forgiveness, which provided him with the energy to return to his father and receive his love and forgiveness. The decision to forgive himself was the critical turning point in his conversion.

If self-forgiveness plays such an important role in the effectiveness of forgiving and healing, why are people so slow to forgive themselves? Here are some reasons why. First, there is an element of self-hatred, anger, or disappointment with oneself for having done wrong. This attitude against oneself needs to be turned around, from being self-destructive to being constructive. This is the key to turning negative energy into a positive power. Another reason is perfectionism, which is a disease that posits an unrealistic expectation of oneself, that one should never fail. Self-forgiveness helps the

Forgiving ourselves will heal the guilt which can cripple us.

perfectionist move from unrealistic expectations to realistic expectations. These include the possibility and the probability of failure in one's life, but also the ability to acquire knowledge from the failure so that the perfectionist grows and becomes a better person.

A third reason is a sense of false pride or conceit, and an inflated sense of self, which considers oneself beyond failure and sin. Self-forgiveness helps such a person to be truthful with himself about his human frailties, limitations, and sinfulness, and to accept himself as he is: flawed. If God always forgives us, then who are we that we refuse to forgive ourselves? A fourth reason is an erroneous belief that self-forgiveness too easily removes the consequences of one's misbehavior and even condones that behavior. Rather, self-forgiveness assists us in facing the reality of our misbehavior, which hurts others and ourselves, and urges us to make reparation and restitution. Self-forgiveness helps us to be more responsible and more accountable for our misbehavior.

A fifth reason is the difficulty some people have in accepting forgiveness, and especially self-forgiveness. This difficulty is often rooted in the absence of the experience of forgiveness in one's family of origin. There may have been an unforgiving and critical atmosphere in the family, leaving people unfamiliar with the experience or expression of forgiveness, or even the consideration of forgiveness. Self-forgiveness helps us transcend the past and break the unhealthy generational cycle of unexpressed forgiveness.

A sixth reason is being overwhelmed by or stuck in guilt and shame. Only forgiving ourselves will heal the guilt and shame that can cripple us. With self-forgiveness we can begin to let go of guilt and shame and move on, experiencing a more kindly attitude toward ourselves.

When we condemn ourselves we lock ourselves up in our sin and immobilize ourselves. We have pity parties. By remaining in a state of self-condemnation we refuse to take the responsibility of forgiving ourselves, of healing, of moving on with our lives, and changing. Some people prefer this state and do not want to be healed. Beating up on themselves makes them more self-centered. The focus is on *my* pain, *my* failure, and *myself*. It becomes a neurotic way of living.

Self-condemnation is useless, but honest criticism of our behavior by ourselves is healthy. The hope is that we can learn who we are from our sins and failures, and acquire valuable information about ourselves in order to bring about change and necessary adjustments in our lives. The decision to forgive ourselves will set us free and enable us to move out of being self-centered victims, depressed and hopeless.

Forgiving oneself doesn't mean we can forget what we have done. The memories will continue to be with us. Those memories, with all their difficult feelings, need to be worked through and sorted out, not buried, denied, or avoided. The decision to forgive oneself opens the door, allowing our painful feelings to flow through us. We need to give ourselves permission to feel everything and anything. Then the emotional healing aspect of the process of self-forgiveness begins. It is a painfully long journey, involving identifying, sorting out, walking through, and talking about our difficult feelings, with God and others, until those feelings are understood, healed, and diffused.

Frequently, repeating the decision to forgive ourselves helps us to absorb these painful feelings. We need to talk to ourselves in a very positive way, to be affirming, to be compassionate and kind to ourselves. Even though we feel badly about our sin, our failure, we know intellectually we have forgiven ourselves.

Eventually, after having achieved intellectual acceptance of self-forgiveness, we will arrive at an emotional acceptance. The feelings will have receded and been diffused. They will no longer be nagging at us, or pulling us back.

Forgiving Others

After forgiving ourselves we are called to forgive others. Sometimes people have a tendency to be casual and superficial about forgiving others. Forgiveness can become a non-reflective act and routine rather than something done with deliberate intent, reflection, and sincerity. To forgive we need to be fully conscious of what the act means, of how we feel, and of what we are thinking. There is always a process operating with forgiveness whether it is done after a slight hurt or a serious hurt. We need to be conscious of this process. A teenage girl once said to me: "Why is Mom always so cranky with Dad? I heard her quickly forgive him after he forgot her birthday. She forgives very quickly." This is an example of unprocessed forgiving in which one slides into forgiveness too quickly, without much reflection.

The elder son in the parable of the prodigal son is a person with whom we can identify. He is hurt and angry. He is having a difficult time forgiving his brother. This elder son often receives a lot of bad press in literature and in sermons because he is slow to forgive, but he shows how difficult it can be to forgive others. He is a good guy. We certainly can identify with him in our own struggles to forgive.

Forgiving is a volitional act, an act of the will, a choice, a decision, even a wish to forgive—all this, even though I don't feel like forgiving. Strong and intense negative feelings about forgiving don't cancel our decision.

Forgiving is a process that begins in the will and then moves through the emotions and is finalized in the spirit. It can be a long process. I need to give myself (and others) the time needed to come to forgiveness. We need to forgive others first for our own sake and then for the others. I need to forgive in order to get myself stabilized and able to release and resolve the negative and difficult feelings that consume me, and that can cause me emotional or physical harm and affect my relationship with others. To forgive others who have offended me is an act of self-love.

"I forgive you, but I'm still angry and hurt." This may sound contradictory, but it is not. The fact is I do forgive you, but I am still full of hostile feelings which I must eventually face and resolve. All this is normal for a person to feel who forgives after being hurt by another. Forgiveness works, but within a normal, human, psychological process. Unless we understand this ambivalence between our decision to forgive and our hostile feelings, we will have conflicts within ourselves about our being good people. We may question whether we have really forgiven the other person because of these hostile feelings. This may be very uncomfortable for a while, but the consoling thought is that we have forgiven the other person, and we are willing to continue and complete the process of forgiveness.

It is important to remember this principle: forgiving doesn't mean forgetting. I can forgive you here and now, but forgetting may take a long time, maybe a lifetime. That's okay, but I need to continue the journey of forgiveness and work through painful areas for my own sake. To continue to repeat the words of forgiveness and to pray for the other person can be helpful in maintaining the decision to forgive. I need to stay with the process for as long as it takes. There are no shortcuts.

EMOTIONAL FORGIVENESS

After volitional forgiveness has been achieved the process of forgiveness continues into the stage of emotional forgiveness. It is a critical aspect of forgiveness. People tend to become stuck here or they may try to shorten it, minimize it, or bypass it altogether. But we need to give ourselves permission to feel. This opens the doors to processing our feelings. We need to be able to feel anything and everything without guilt or shame, whether the feelings involved are logical or illogical.

One of the main reasons we don't complete the forgiving process is our anger. This, in turn, prevents us from facing and dealing with the hurts, frustrations, and fears underneath our anger. Feeling angry does not mean we are bad people. We acknowledge that we are hurt, and this allows us to get inside our hurt. Feeling angry toward another doesn't mean we don't also have some loving feelings toward the person. We probably have ambivalent feelings. Hurt and anger are all part of relationships, even intimate ones. As our anger is resolved and diffused the feelings of love will reappear. If they don't appear then the relationship may have to be evaluated even more closely, perhaps because of the nature of the hurt.

Unresolved and buried feelings, especially anger, will destroy a relationship. Unrecognized resentment can appear in many destructive ways that will undermine a relationship. In healthy relationships people talk out their hurt and anger as well as their other feelings. One of them might say: "I forgive you, but I am still hurt and angry

Emotional forgiveness leads to deeper knowledge of one another.

about what you did to me." Gradually, as people talk their feelings out with one another, painful feelings are diffused. A better, mutual understanding occurs, and the relationship heals and grows. Emotional forgiveness actually leads people to a deeper knowledge of one another.

When an offended party feels rage and hate toward another, the offended one will usually have to soften and diffuse these intense feelings first. Then, when rage and hate have become appropriate anger, he or she will be able to express this to the other. Sometimes feelings may be so intense that it will be necessary for one to talk them out with a trusted friend or counselor, to be able to speak to the offender in a reasonable way while expressing appropriate feelings. It is a matter of taking one's energy and using it in a constructive way.

Sometimes, underneath the hurt and anger are other unresolved hurts and angry feelings that have not yet been dealt with. One offense may have surfaced other unresolved offenses. Then we have a cascade of issues and feelings that need to be sorted out. The danger of not facing up to life's hurts is that they don't go away, but come back to make matters worse. Sometimes people are amazed at the amount of anger they have expressed toward a person who hurt them, only to realize that underneath that one hurt are many other unresolved hurts. To avoid overreaction we need to distinguish the present hurt from other hurts that have not been resolved. Then we can address the other hurts.

Emotional forgiveness is the link between intellectual forgiveness—the decision to forgive—and spiritual forgiveness—letting go. People have a tendency to go from the decision to forgive to the letting go, and avoid facing up to their feelings. This is not genuine forgiveness because the relevant feelings have not been resolved. Beware of people who quickly forgive us and deny any hurt, but don't speak to us the next day. They are feeling resentment because the unresolved hurt and anger were not dealt with—hence, there is no genuine forgiveness. It's better for them to say: "I forgive you, but

I need time to deal with my hurt and with other difficult feelings I have in regard to what you did."

Whether it is a matter of a slight or a serious hurt the process I have described is always necessary. There will always be lesser or greater feelings to face. In either case, whether it takes a few minutes, a few weeks, or years the feelings need to be acknowledged, accepted, and addressed; and, if necessary, expressed appropriately.

All this being said, we can understand why the act of forgiveness is an art. Its practice is an absolute necessity for everyone if they are to heal and grow emotionally and spiritually.

Spiritual Forgiveness or Letting Go

As the journey of emotional forgiveness comes to an end, the process of forgiveness leads us into spiritual forgiveness, which involves letting go, letting God, and moving on with our lives.

The goal in the process of forgiveness is to arrive at spiritual forgiveness. Some people arrive there quickly. Others are slower, and still others may never arrive, but that's OK. As long as we continue to work with our emotions we are moving in the right direction. Sexually abused people are an example of how it may take a lifelong journey to resolve the feelings they have toward their abuser.

Letting go is primarily for our own sake in order to rid ourselves of any painful baggage, which, if unattended, will harm us emotionally and physically. That baggage can control our lives if we let it. We'll never be free if we carry these unresolved hurt feelings and negative thoughts around with us. They will continue to affect us and torment us.

Besides the abundant psychological evidence that forgiveness brings emotional and spiritual healing, we also have mounting medical evidence today of the physical healing forgiveness brings. Michael Torosian and Veruschka Biddle, in their encouraging book *Spirit to Heal: A Journey to Spiritual Healing with Cancer*, speak of the power of forgiveness to heal us physically.

Forgiveness is so powerful that it can immediately release blocked emotions. Often our mind perceives that a particular emotion has gone away, but intense emotions once stored in the body will not resolve or disappear by repressing or denying them. Forgiveness is a

Forgiveness is so powerful it can release blocked emotions.

powerful way of releasing negative emotions and the entire experience associated with them. When we are released from that pain, we experience a peace and freedom the world cannot provide in any other way.

Letting go doesn't mean condoning the other person's act, or absolving them, or forgetting how they have offended us. It doesn't mean ignoring the consequences of their hurtful behavior. We may trust them or we may never trust them again. The relationship may be the same, better, or worse—or it may end. But I am not holding on to all that negative energy. I am a free person, able to choose. It's like letting go of a helium balloon. It goes up, up, and away until eventually I can't see it anymore.

Letting go can mean mercy, compassion, and understanding, but never denial that the particular offense occurred. Sometimes we forgive those who have hurt us not out of justice, but mercy. We must remember that this type of letting go will be valid only if we have walked the painful journey of forgiveness. The offender needs to respect the offended person's need for time before forgiveness can be attained. He must not pressure her. This approach is common among men who grow anxious and impatient and begin to pressure their wives to trust them before the wives are ready to trust. Men attempt to initiate sex at such a time even though their wives are not ready emotionally. These men are not listening, which is probably part of the overall problem in their relationship with their wives. A husband's trustworthiness can be proven by changing his behavior, and being open and honest while listening to his wife.

A marital relationship may or may not return to a better level of trust, but the partners need to give the relationship a chance to work. If they both try, they will always have a sense of satisfaction that they did all they could to achieve resolution and reconciliation.

Finally, letting go means moving on with our lives and with our relationships. We have forgiven, and so a great millstone has been lifted from our necks. We are free to move forward. It is futile to refuse to forgive another in order to punish him. In the long run we are only self-destructively punishing ourselves, because we are immobilizing ourselves emotionally and spiritually. We need to forgive others first for our own sake in order to heal.

The spirituality of letting go gives us the possibility, in our relationship, of communicating better, listening more effectively, and seeing our differences more clearly. We can move on together to a closer and more mature relationship.

Moving on is also about resurrection, breaking out of the tomb of bitterness by our act of forgiveness. We will realize we have moved on to another level of living. We have become better people, not bitter people. Good things happen to us when we journey through the forgiving process.

RECONCILIATION

People often confuse forgiveness with reconciliation and perceive them as synonymous. But they are two different concepts. Forgiveness is a process of letting go. Reconciliation means healing, and putting the broken relationship back together. Without forgiveness there can never be any genuine reconciliation.

There are three outcomes that can occur within a relationship after one party has forgiven the other. The first is that the partners not only reconcile but there's the possibility that the relationship can become more intimate because the parties concerned have shared in the process of forgiving, deeply and emotionally. They have come to better know and understand each other. Forgiveness, in this case, has become a bonding force. The offended and the offender lay out their differences openly and honestly. The resolution of disagreements is not achieved by avoiding, controlling or submitting, but by uniting two opposites together by compromise, cooperation, and tolerance. We often refer to this process as "reconciling differences."

Trust is the foundation of an intimate, loving relationship, but trust is strengthened through the act of forgiveness that rises out of the hurts and conflicts in people's relationships. At such a vulnerable time the painful sharing that occurs makes people known to one another so that the mutual revelation of each other often results in resolution.

People in close relationships need to be realistic and realize that they will hurt and disappoint each other at times, but one hopes they will forgive each other. It is only through such interaction that relationships grow; otherwise they will remain stagnant.

If reconciliation is to occur, forgiveness always needs to be verbalized. For either party to assume or presume that forgiveness has occurred is too tenuous, and often leaves people in doubt about whether they have been forgiven.

A second outcome of forgiveness may be that even after one party in a relationship has forgiven the other, the relationship may not be the same as before. The offended person has forgiven the other, but the offended party remains cool and distant with the other. The act of forgiveness is genuine, but trust has been damaged. Because of the nature of the offense—for example, unfaithfulness, persistent lying, or emotional abuse—there will be sense of loss, of hurt. When trust is restored a relationship may go back to what it was, may be better than it was, or neither.

A third possibility in the area of reconciliation is that, even after forgiveness has been accepted, there can be no reconciliation. Forgiveness doesn't always mean reconciliation. It is a sad fact, but not all relationships can be put back together. Relationships where there has been severe physical, emotional, or sexual abuse are usually beyond repair and, for their own safety, the victims should not even consider reconciliation.

Victims of abuse need to understand why they chose the partners they did and why they remained in an unhealthy relationship. In such cases, leaving the partner is an external change, but the internal psychological and spiritual change is even more necessary so that the victim can move on into a life of healthy relationships.

We need to be aware of the ambivalent feelings that are a normal part of severing a relationship with another. People may have spent a long time together, experienced many years of sharing good times and bad. It takes time to sever the nerve endings of a former relationship. In our head and heart we know we can never trust the other person again—a sad and disappointing realization. But there can be no more denial: the relationship is over in spite of all our mixed feelings. Some relationships die and others should never have been.

Ending a relationship can cause a deep sense of loss, even though we may feel relieved and know that this ending is for the best. We need to allow ourselves to grieve over the loss of a relationship. The hopes and dreams we had for the relationship will never be attained. The ramifications of this loss will involve other connected losses that are part and parcel of lost relationships. We can't move on with life or in another close relationship until we have fully explored and resolved the lost relationship, asking how we failed each other.

We forgive others for our own sake.

In some broken relationships one person wants the relationship to work and resists the decision of the other person to leave. This is extremely painful for the person who is seeking to heal the relationship, but after making many fruitless attempts at reconciliation, he or she needs to accept and deal with the reality that the relationship is over. It takes two willing and motivated people to make any relationship work. A relationship in which one person opts to leave can't be made to work.

Sometimes people in irreconcilable relationships struggle with the question as to whether or not they should verbalize their forgiveness to the other person. In their head and heart, and with a trusted friend, they have verbalized their forgiveness of the other person. But it is not necessary to tell the offender this in order to make the forgiveness valid. In cases of sexual or physical abuse, verbalized forgiveness may make us vulnerable to unfair and unwarranted comments from the other or it may be perceived as condoning their behavior. It may also be misinterpreted as suggesting the possibility of reconciling, or that we are at fault.

People will need to make a calculated judgment as to whether verbalized forgiveness will be beneficial to themselves and the other person, or a detriment. The answer is not always clear-cut, and erring on the side of caution is the more judicious thing to do. There may be times when we need to tell the other person directly that we have forgiven him or her, for example, the offender is dying and needs to hear it. However, this decision to verbalize our forgiveness needs to be made at the appropriate time, and for sound reasons and with healthy emotions: without guilt, shame, compulsion, or impulsiveness.

The question often arises, who should take the initiative to forgive and to be reconciled? The answer is this: the offender must take the initiative and ask for forgiveness and for reconciliation. Jesus gives this example "If you bring your gift to the altar and there you recall that your brother or sister has something against you, leave your gift at the altar, go first and be reconciled with your brother and sister, and then return to the altar" (Matthew 5:23–24). Jesus also states that we must forgive "seventy times seven"—which is code language for again and again.

Jesus goes a step further in his teaching when he encourages us to take the initiative to forgive and to be reconciled, even when we are the offended one. "If your brother or sister should commit some wrong against you, go and point out the fault, but keep it between the two of you. If your brother or sister listens to you, you have won them over" (Matthew 18:15). Jesus continues: if the offender refuses our forgiveness and call for reconciliation, let them go. We have done what we could and can be at peace with ourselves. Jesus left us a striking example of his words about forgiveness when, on the cross, he said: "Father, forgive them for they do not know what they are doing" (Luke 23:34). Jesus also encourages us to pray for our enemies, for those who persecute or hate us, and for all difficult people who don't like us or whom we don't like.

The question that Jesus puts before all of us is: "Do you want to be healed?" (John 5:6). If we say yes, then we must be willing to take the necessary steps toward healing. An essential point in the finding of this healing is the willingness to forgive and to be forgiven. Forgiving doesn't mean forgetting. We need to forgive others primarily for our own sake and then for theirs.

Forgiveness doesn't always mean that reconciliation with others will be possible. These fundamental truths about the act of forgiveness will set us free to forgive, and to become the persons God has destined us to be.

7.

Life's Losses

Life is full of losses. From womb to tomb, a series of losses follows us through life. Losses are a normal, frequent, and difficult part of living and growing up. Some losses are more shocking, painful, and frustrating than others. When we consider the losses of life we are amazed at their various dimensions, aspects, and nuances.

A major criterion for emotionally healthy and wholesome living is the ability of a person to identify losses as soon as possible when they occur, and then face them and resolve their emotional content by moving through them, adjusting, accepting, letting go, and moving on. Whether losses we suffer are minor, like the loss of a chance to have lunch with a friend, or major, like the loss of a powerful and financially lucrative position in a company, no one is free from losses.

Life's losses can be placed in six general categories. First, there is the death of loved ones such as parents, spouses, and children, with all the resultant losses that are the consequences of the death of a loved one. We include here the death of a cherished pet.

Second, there are damaged or lost relationships, as happens in divorce or in the breakup of a close friendship, with all the repercussions connected with the breakup, such as the loss of relatives, holiday celebrations, and sexual relations.

Third, there are the family losses we experience, for example, the alcoholic father who is not present to the family emotionally or who abandons his family, thus being lost to them; or there are the parents who never expressed their love, affection, and affirmation to their children; or there are the parents who were constantly ill, or physically or emotionally debilitated and thus not able to parent.

Fourth, there are the dreaded tragedies that strike without warning, like a car accident that leaves one paralyzed; or being fired; or the loss of a large sum of money in a business deal gone bad; or a miscarriage; or financial loss in the stock market.

Fifth, there are the daily losses of life such as disappointment in one's children; unmet expectations; dreams unfulfilled; the disloyalty of a trusted friend; or the missed opportunities to do a good deed or to speak up at a meeting; or the loss of one's self-esteem, respect, dignity, or good name. Then there's the picnic that is rained out, the home team losing a football game; there's the loss of youth, with attendant loss of hearing or sight, or the general diminishing of good health and the loss of sexual energy and interest.

Sixth, there are the necessary losses, such as the removal of a cancerous organ to save one's life; or the leaving of a physical and emotionally abusive relationship in order to protect oneself; or the leaving of a good job and co-workers for a better salary and position.

The point I want to make is that sometimes the losses we experience are not always recognized because they can be quite subtle. The more we can identify our losses the more we can process them and so keep ourselves emotionally and spiritually alive and healthy. Indeed losses are painful, but when we address them they are all opportunities for personal and spiritual growth.

Many of our experiences of loss are common experiences to

which we can all relate. They connect all of us in the human condition. When we are mourning with our family and friends at the graveside of someone we all loved, we share with different intensity in sadness and in the painful feelings of loss. There are losses that reach back into infancy, as when a baby is weaned from its mother's breast or when a child cries over the loss of her teddy bear. There are the many good-byes of life that are more or less difficult. There is the loss of a tooth or the loss of one's hair, or a cherished memento is misplaced.

Changes involve losing and letting go in order to grow.

There are the falling leaves which mean the end of summer. The path through life is littered with losses and we are constantly challenged to adjust to them.

Some losses are so insignificant that we feel embarrassed to admit any feelings of loss. Nonetheless they are losses and need to be acknowledged—at least to ourselves. No loss should go unrecognized. Even when no one understands our loss or recognizes that we're experiencing one, that loss will always be important to us in the silent recesses of our hearts.

Losses are inherent in the human condition. They are either good or bad, fair or unfair, but they are realities in our daily lives. Some losses are an integral part of the progression of life; the child has to leave the security of home to begin kindergarten; the high school student has to leave his family to begin college; children have to learn how to lose a ballgame and that learning to lose is as important as learning how to win; the teenager has to let go of her teens and enter into adulthood. There's the common aging process we all experience, especially old age, which often means the loss of physical and mental competence.

Gail Sheehy, in her book *Passages*, describes the crises and changes of adult life as opportunities for creative change from which people emerge stronger than they were. It is a matter of giving up one thing to gain another, e.g., leaving the academic atmosphere of the university for the competition of the business world. Sometimes it can mean giving up certain ways of behaving in favor of more mature behavior. Or it might mean my not being satisfied with who I am and becoming a better person. Some people in their late twenties are still emotionally adolescent because they will not let go of certain behaviors or dependencies.

Changes in our lives always involve losing and letting go in order to grow. In her book *Necessary Losses*, Judith Viorst writes about "how we grow and change through the losses that are an inevitable and necessary part of life, the loves, illusions, dependencies, and impossible expectations that all of us have to give up in order to grow."

There are three stages in the journey through loss. First, there is the acknowledgment of the reality of the loss. This helps one to overcome shock, disbelief, and denial, or minimizing or pretending about the loss. Second, there is the walk through the sadness and all the other painful feelings loss brings. Third, one accepts the loss, lets go, and moves on with life. Depending on the nature of the loss, this process can last a few seconds, hours, days, weeks, or years.

Acknowledging the Loss

When we acknowledge and deal with the reality of losses in our life we can become more reality-oriented. Facing reality always keeps us honest and mentally healthy. It also sensitizes us more to the losses that others experience. It makes us more human and compassionate people when we experience the pain, sorrow, and frustration of our losses.

Whether our losses seem significant or not, they are all losses and need to be addressed and processed, because each loss is a stepping-stone on the journey through life. The more we identify the loss, the more we weaken the walls of denial and the less we rationalize about the loss and pretend it didn't happen, the more easily shock and disbelief will disappear and we will face the painful reality of the loss. This is one way we mature emotionally and spiritually.

Parents can prepare children for life when they teach and assist them to face and deal with their daily losses and failures, big or small. When parents avoid dealing with their children's losses and with the pain and frustration they bring, they slow their children's emotional and spiritual development. Of course, one must ask what the parents' behavior says about their ability to deal with losses in their own life.

The more we are aware of, sensitive to, and respectful of our own losses, the more we can take ownership and responsibility for them. We will be credible when we say to another, "I know what you are going through." People can be terribly insensitive to other people's losses because they are unaware of their own.

SADNESS OVER THE LOSS

Sadness over a loss is the stage of feeling that ushers us into a time of grieving with a greater or a lesser amount of pain, depending on the importance of our loss. Since grieving is painful, we have a natural tendency to want to avoid it or in some way minimize the painful feelings. The student who fails an exam tells his friend who inquires how he feels about the failure, "It was only an exam. No big deal." Isn't this typical of how people frequently deal with loss? They casually skip over them with little or no emotional experience or expression of their loss, but they are hurting inside, whether they realize it or not. Such suppression causes them to be a little less human, less in touch with their inner world of feelings. They continue to stack away unresolved feelings and so become insensitive to life.

Some people make every loss in their lives, whether lesser or greater, an emotional disaster. They lack a sense of proportion and overreact. They often get stuck in one loss after another and never complete any grieving at all. They tend to be gloomy and negative, in a constant state of mourning. They are extremely insecure and lack self-confidence. They can become bitter, and become professional victims. But if we identify our losses and pass through them we won't become stuck emotionally, or depressed, gloomy, unhappy, or bitter. People who are mired in their losses can be unaware that they are stuck, emotionally paralyzed.

Sadness may be difficult but it is not necessarily a bad feeling. It is painful, but it tells us that we have lost something important and dear to us. Depression, however, is an overwhelming state of mind. Depression is buried sadness, buried with all the other feelings that go with grieving. In sadness we can still function and go on with our

Relief and sadness can go together.

lives; depression causes us to be dysfunctional. We are often not able to function in our daily lives.

Underneath most people's depression I have found much unresolved grief over losses in their lives. Sometimes people will feel ashamed of such feelings or think they are being selfish for feeling that way about themselves. Actually, they need to allow themselves to be human and to experience those feelings. When we grieve over our losses, we can build character, and character is about how we deal with the losses of life. The main reason people don't know how to grieve is that they don't know how to feel, or don't allow themselves to feel.

Ambivalent feelings about a loss are a frequent experience. A woman may feel joy and relief that the tumor in her breast is not cancerous, but will also feel sad about the possible disfigurement of her body. There may be relief that the family dog died after a serious illness, but also tears of sadness that the animal is gone. Relief and sadness can go together. To feel relief is not bad, but a normal feeling for the good of the dog as well as for the family that has been suffering as it saw the animal in pain.

People can confuse being unemotional and unexpressive of grief with being a strong person, when really such stoicism is a weakness and denial of our being fully human. Such people fear their feelings; they fear pain; they feel uncomfortable with their feelings. They don't understand that sad feelings are a necessary aspect of grieving. They don't know how to deal with their feelings so they avoid or bury them, thinking that this is the way to control them, when actually, their feelings are controlling them. They may make light of their loss or joke about it in order not to feel or appear weak. All of these tactics prevent them from grieving appropriately and so they cannot heal.

Sometimes people are insensitive to and unsupportive of others' grief. They avoid dealing with a grieving person because they feel uncomfortable and don't know what to say or do. They may also think of the loss as insignificant or silly, and joke about it or brush it aside. They often mean well, but aggravate the person's pain with insensitive remarks such as, "You shouldn't feel so bad about selling the car. It was only a car. You can get another one. You'll be OK tomorrow." People would be much more helpful by feeling with the person and just listening to her and letting her talk and feel. The person knows she can buy another car, but she needs to deal with the loss of this "old faithful" car.

Why is it that so many women feel sad and even depressed after a miscarriage? They have suffered a severe loss and need to grieve but are frequently met with the insensitive comment, "Don't feel bad— you can get pregnant again." Useless advice! What they need is our support and encouragement to grieve.

If women need to grieve over a miscarriage, it is also imperative that those who have had an abortion grieve. Abortion is not just a medical procedure after which life goes on as usual. It is a choice by the woman, and, in many situations, with the consent of her mate or because of his pressuring her. The deep physical, emotional, mental, and spiritual pain that pierces the soul of both the woman and the man are incalculable. There is a sense of relief for them, right after the abortion, but eventually, the loss will have to be faced. There is underlying pain that won't go away. It cannot be denied or repressed.

Over the years I have had the privilege of counseling many hurting women and men who worked through the pain of the abortion, sought forgiveness, forgave themselves, and named their child. They owned their abortion. It was a process of emotional and spiritual growth and healing. I mentioned men who have been involved in their partner's abortion because they often feel left out of the grieving process for the child, or have been in denial about what happened. These men also need to grieve, heal, seek forgiveness, and forgive themselves. There is a group called Project Rachel where people who have unresolved abortion issues can find safe haven, healing, and hope. Remember, God's love and compassion are limitless.

ACCEPTANCE AND RESOLUTION OF LOSS

We have faced the reality of loss and walked our way through our sadness and other connecting feelings. Now we terminate our grieving by entering the stage of acceptance and resolution, letting go, and moving on with our lives. The recovery process brought us to healing. We may not be fully healed, but at least the process is beginning and we are moving on.

Acceptance doesn't mean we like or approve of our loss, but we are willing to live with the reality of it. For example, "The old boss is leaving us. He did a good job and served us well. We will miss him." Gradually the pain of losing him ebbs away outside of an occasional feeling about him that we may have. Memories of what or whom we have lost will occasionally return and maybe some consequences will remain from our losses, but healing will be taking place because we have addressed our loss, and met it head-on. We have made changes and other adaptations. We are at peace with ourselves. We've let go, and, in faith and trust, put it all in God's hands. We can move on with our lives.

Life may be different in many ways because of our loss. We are much wiser in our judgment of others. There are no more millstones of unresolved painful feelings around our neck pulling us down. We realize that to complete our grieving over a loss, we must go from the reality of the loss through the painful feelings before arriving at a final acceptance and resolution. We move on. There are no shortcuts. We can't go from reality to acceptance. We need to go through the painful area of dealing with the emotional pain, which will eventually be diffused if we face it.

Some losses in life are so tragic that grieving and healing will be a lifelong process, for example, when people are physically debilitated by the loss of an arm. Grieving over the loss and healing will continue throughout their lives. Some people are suffering from terminal illnesses; they are dying by inches. Their grieving is a daily process. They need to continue to live through the different levels of the reality of their illness, the painful feelings that go with it, and the acceptance of the illness.

How do people grieve and survive a cascade of losses? It requires, among other things, living one day at a time and focusing on the main issues of that day, and prioritizing which issues need to be addressed, when. Some problems need to be put aside and dealt with later; we must recognize our limitations. Nor can we expect to process all our feelings for every loss at the same time. Some feelings will have to be stored—not repressed—until there is time to process them.

We need to keep our expectations realistic, and reassure ourselves that all issues will require time to be processed. There are no quick and fast solutions. We need to be compassionate, patient, and understanding with ourselves.

We will need to have support people with whom we can vent our feelings and talk about our problems in order to make adjustments and find possible solutions. Counseling can be of great assistance; indeed, for some people counseling will be absolutely necessary. We need to take care of ourselves physically, emotionally, mentally, and spiritually if we expect to make it through all these losses. I have seen many people go through a series of losses and come out better, happier, and more confident people.

Self-confidence implies that, no matter what losses I sustain, I will be able to deal with them in one way or another. Frequently people find new resources within themselves they never realized they had. The CEO of a large, successful company loses his position, only to become a successful real estate agent which pays better than his former position did.

I need to reach out for help, and find and surface the resources that are available to help me. Not becoming overwhelmed is important for survival and healing.

8.

Loss of a Significant Relationship

The loss of a close relationship, especially a relationship with a spouse, can be equally as painful and stressful as the death of a loved one. In fact, many who have experienced both claim that the death of the spousal relationship, especially through divorce, is even more agonizing than the death of a spouse. In either case these losses are two of the most stressful experiences in life.

With the death of a spouse, we realize the person is gone. In the death of a relationship the other person is still alive and, especially in a divorce, the former spouse is still "around." If there are children, there will be a certain amount of unavoidable contact. Even when children are not involved there are still times, like family gatherings or funerals or random meetings, at which contact with a former spouse is unavoidable. With each contact old wounds, as well as both joyful and sad memories, often flash before the divorced person's eyes. The divorce does not always bring physical closure. Divorced couples are still quite vulnerable when they meet. Similar dynamics are present in any broken relationship.

I repeat: even though my remarks here will be focused on divorce, the same dynamics will be experienced by anyone in a broken relationship, especially if it was a close or intimate relationship. Whether these relationships are between children, teens, adults, or senior citizens, the same emotional pain will be experienced. Close relationships can be between persons of all ages and walks of life, between family members and between members of the same sex.

When emotional, intimate relationships disintegrate beyond repair, people experience the same pain and stages of grieving that accompany the end of irreconcilable relationships. Only the degree of the emotional intensity of the hurt will differ. Whatever the length or quality such relationships, denial or pretending there is no hurt or sense of loss is not an option if we wish to truly heal emotionally and spiritually.

Grieving

The termination of any close relationship, no matter how brief and superficial, requires grieving. It is commonly believed that long-standing relationships such as those in marriage, and even more temporary involvements, are mourned when they end, while the breakup of lesser relationships, or of children or teens' relationships are viewed as passing experiences that should know little pain or disappointment. We consider such relationships as insignificant and think that the persons involved will get over hurt quickly.

Parents need to be aware of their children's broken friendships so they can teach the children to acknowledge their hurt and pain, and to resolve that hurt and pain by talking about what happened and letting the children express their feelings. When parents neglect to attach any importance to such events in their children's lives, children learn to treat such painful experiences as unimportant. They

Every broken relationship needs to be grieved over.

bury their hurt and go on with their lives, but they are thus robbed of learning how to face the common, normal breakup of relationships, which will occur again in their lives. When the children's experience of broken relationships is not taken seriously by parents, children are deprived of the chance to know themselves better and to learn lessons from the failed friendship, information that can be vital to them when they come to build better and stronger relationships in the future.

Teenagers and young adults frequently go in and out of emotionally intense but brief relationships. Sometimes the young may seem quite superficial when a relationship collapses, for they usually don't process the loss or reflect on what happened to them sufficiently. They bury their feelings and involve themselves in other emotional attachments. In such cases, their emotional wounds go untreated and the young miss an opportunity of learning from the experience. Underneath much of our young people's turmoil and depression are feelings of hurt, anger, disappointment, and anxiety about the lost relationship that have not been worked through and resolved.

We must cease seeing our children and teenagers as being without emotional pain in the areas of broken friendships, and acknowledge that they too have feelings. Granted, their relationships may be superficial and immature; nonetheless their wounded feelings are a reality. At times adults are not in touch with their own hurt feelings, so they tend to be in denial about the pain and hurt their children may be experiencing. The basic principle is that every broken relationship needs to be acknowledged and properly grieved over, even those relationships which should cease. Otherwise, future relationships will be jeopardized. Parents need to help their children talk about their broken relationships and not make light of them by saying, for example: "You'll find another girlfriend soon."

Every failed relationship encourages us to confront and question our style of relating to others. In every relationship that fails there are always two aspects to the failure. How did the relationship fail? and, How did I fail in the relationship? Failed relationships can lead us to deeper levels of emotional and spiritual maturity. A broken relationship can challenge us to find the courage to seek and develop better and healthier relationships.

Much has been written about the characteristics of healthy, mature relationships. However, we need to know how to survive and learn from failed relationships. We need to emerge from them as better persons—not bitter, not cynical. Therefore we all need to reflect on our failed relationships so that we are not only healed but also informed and transformed by painful experiences. We need to realize that failing in relationships is part of life, but that we can move on without being destroyed. Further, we must learn to take responsibility for our part in why a relationship failed.

Dealing with broken relationships means facing the reality of what happened; experiencing and talking about that reality and the feelings that came with it; and eventually letting go and moving on. We will not be able to have good relationships with everyone. We can develop close relationships with only a few people. Sometimes we create much unnecessary suffering in our lives because of unrealistic expectations that we have to be friends with everyone.

The Harsh Reality of Divorce

Of all broken relationships divorce is the most prominent and most painful of all. We know how many marriages fail. This has become a social and religious concern because of the devastation divorce causes to spouses, their children, and the extended family, not to mention the harm it does to society as a whole. Divorce can be a financial and emotional disaster.

Hardly a family exists that has not experienced the tragic effect of divorce. Because it is such a common phenomenon, more easily attained today than in the past, and more acceptable, many people conclude that people divorce quickly and without much thought and reflection. As one who has listened to the painful stories of divorcing people for over thirty years, I can say that such suppositions are not true. The majority of divorced people that I have worked with go through an agonizing experience that can be compared to the agony of Jesus in the Garden: "Father, if it is possible, remove this cup from me."

Divorce is not taken lightly by most people. They may threaten divorce, they may talk about it, but it is not a journey that people embark upon quickly and without anguish. In fact, sometimes people stay in a marriage that has turned sour for a time far beyond what they should because they do not want to admit failure and to enter the agony of the divorcing process. The fears and the anxiety of the unknown future, especially about living alone, haunt them.

Sometimes a spouse screams "I want a divorce" in a fit of frustration, but they often mean that they don't want to live in the type of miserable relationship they are in. Often people choose divorce impulsively without realizing there can be alternatives. For example, a couple could seek counseling, cool off, discuss their differences calmly, perhaps obtain some intervention, some mediation. Married people sometimes don't realize that marriage is a difficult proposition in which there will be differences and problems, and all that is part of the process of achieving a better relationship. To paraphrase David Schnarck: marriage is difficult, but the problems and anxieties that come with it can help people grow. And when people grow, relationships grow.

At times divorcing spouses sitting in a divorce court wonder how it all came to this. Once lawyers are called into the picture the adversarial aspect of divorce begins and, eventually, takes over. There is no stopping this rolling stone that is divorce down the legal hill. Many people regret that they did not seek counseling before divorcing. Actually, seeking a divorce without getting counseling is tantamount to crossing a busy street with one's eyes closed when one could go to the corner and wait for the light. In fact, a counselor is as important as a lawyer.

Counseling will allow people to work their way through many difficulties, and especially through the emotional labyrinth they are sure to encounter. Often counseling will make it all the more obvious that a marriage cannot be saved and probably should not have taken place. The spouses can then walk away from the counseling sessions with the realization that they did all they could to save the marriage and that reconciliation is not possible. This process can remove any later haunting doubts that often bother people as to whether or not the marriage could have worked, if they had only "tried harder."

Moving On

People need to feel that a marriage is over so that they can grieve over the death of the marriage, face the consequences, and move on with their lives. Thus will be removed any doubts that the marriage was still viable or not, and open the door for people to grieve over the marriage that has been lost.

All marital problems are two-sided.

One of the misunderstandings people living in troubled marriages have is that if the other partner will not agree to counseling there can be no effective counseling. "What's the use of going to counseling? My husband refuses to go." Ideally, it's best if both spouses come for counseling. In reality, however, frequently the wife is more willing to face painful issues and emotions and to seek counseling on her own. Many marriages have been saved because one spouse was willing to look at himself or herself and change what he or she could change.

All marital problems are two-sided. They are not caused by one person. For example, if one spouse is controlling then the other one is submitting. That in itself presents two sets of problems. Even in the most undesirable situations the victim spouse needs to understand how she is enabling and reinforcing her husband's behavior and how she needs to be more assertive in confronting his inappropriate behavior and/or language. As unfair as her husband may be, she needs to change so that she can begin to break the "sick" patterns of the marriage. She is changing what she can change, which is herself, and at the same time taking more responsibility for herself and for her part in the marriage.

Often women in bad marriages have allowed themselves to accept more responsibility for the marital difficulties then they should. As a result they have not only lost their self-confidence but their sense of self. Counseling can help them regain their self-confidence and be assertive, to take charge of their lives. The results of this are often remarkable; the marriage has changed because the wife has changed.

Because one spouse had the motivation and courage to change, this will have a positive influence on the other spouse's behavior.

A troubled marriage can often be saved when both partners are willing to look at themselves, take responsibility for their behavior, stop blaming each other, and change what they can change in themselves. However, if one person completely refuses to change or work on the marriage, maybe the marriage is over. If only one person is so willing there can be no marriage. The resistant partner may proclaim he wants the marriage to last, but his behavior is negative and controlling. The truth is obvious in his behavior, not in his words. Counseling will then assist the willing partner to come to the realization that the marriage is over and that she should take the legal and emotional steps to dissolve the union.

Even in non-problem marriages both partners are required to be willing to work on themselves and on the relationship. Sometimes spouses remain together for such reasons as children, finances, their parents, and so on, but these situations can be very problematic, causing tension in the family and other emotionally destructive consequences. Fear, guilt, shame, and a host of other feelings and ways of thinking can keep a couple together in a house—but it is not a home.

Divorce is a painful reality that drastically changes people's lives and affects many innocent people, especially children. The marriage is over. This is a shocking realization and the disbelief it engenders takes many forms. Spouses will know intellectually that the marriage is over, but they will cling to it emotionally. There is always that hope that the relationship can be saved. Sometimes it is, for a brief period of time, but eventually the fact must be faced: it's over. Denial, blaming, and pretending are part and parcel of life after divorce, but the reality remains: the marriage is over.

Divorcing people need to be reassured that they will make it through the process. We need to give them a sense of hope that they will come through this ordeal and find healing, that there is life after divorce, but that they will have to traverse a barren desert before they arrive at a final acceptance or resolution. This requires time. There are no short-cuts.

Some years ago I gave a lecture to a group of people who were divorced or separated. The title of my presentation was "The Exodus

Experience." In this presentation I likened the divorce experience to the plight of the Israelites being called out of Egypt to the Promised Land. Divorcing people are often being called by God from a destructive relationship which can no longer be called a marriage because it is no longer life-giving. They are being called to a new life. However, it will take time before the Promised Land can be entered.

Once the reality of the end of the marriage is acknowledged, the painful journey through the feelings of sadness and even craziness begins. Hope of reconciliation disappears. Pleading with the former partner doesn't work. This is a time of great emotional swings, together with a certain disbelief with all that is happening.

ANGER AND DIVORCE

Accompanying the deep sadness connected with most divorces are the strong and at times overwhelming feelings of anger, rage, and even hate. The deep hurt, fear, and frustration connected with a divorce will naturally evoke tremendous anger. This anger or rage is understandable, but it must be talked about. Relatives and friends have to encourage and support the divorcing persons in their anger. The anger needs to be brought to the surface and diffused in a safe atmosphere, such as exists with friends and counselors. But such anger at the other spouse should not be displayed in the presence of any children at this time when the divorcing persons are so explosive.

In a divorce, anger is probably the strongest emotion needing to be addressed. Divorcing persons can become stuck in anger, which makes them unable to move through the divorce process in an appropriate way. If anger and other feelings are suppressed, the divorcing person will become depressed. The other extreme occurs when the divorced person remains in a state of anger. Then, the anger is often displaced on other innocent parties and can be destructive of the person himself. People are turned off by this angry person and begin to avoid him. Anger is controlling his or her life. Such anger gives control to the former spouse, even though the former spouse does not realize it.

Divorce involves an emotional and spiritual journey of grieving. The divorced need to acknowledge that they want to heal. The better they resolve their feelings, the more control they can take of their lives, and, especially of their thinking. Divorced people often make one bad decision after another because their decisions are based on their feelings, and not on sound reason. They have not resolved their emotional turmoil and therefore, often act impulsively because of anger or fear. It's a beautiful thing in counseling to see divorced people working through their feelings and resolving them, and then being able to reason more soundly, to make better decisions in their lives. Difficult feelings are important and need to be addressed, but they should not be allowed to control one's reasoning or decisions.

Sometimes the anger of a divorced person is directed toward people other than the former spouse; for example, toward in-laws, or anyone else who may have been a real or imagined accomplice in the marital breakup. If there was an affair, the third party may be the target of much anger. Indeed, all these other people may have been factors contributing to the divorce. But often they divert the divorced person from facing the real causes of the breakup. The fact is, the marriage failed because two people failed. The main focus of any anger needs to be myself and my spouse. Diverting anger from the spouses to others can keep the divorcing person from facing the true causes of the failure of the marriage, and from facing the fact that the marriage is over and that there is no hope of reconciliation.

The suffering of divorce, especially the hurt and anger, affect the spouse who has been left for another. The subsequent sense of rejection is combined with thoughts of being inadequate and worthless. The futility and frustration felt when one wants to reconcile and work on the marriage but the other person has no intention of or interest in reconciling, are devastating. Perhaps one spouse had been considering divorce for a long time, but he or she never gave any clue to this possibility. Very often spouses who leave a marriage for another person have repressed their discontent with their marriage, burying anger and other negative feelings and thoughts about their partner. This silence may be interpreted by the other spouse as meaning that the other was satisfied and happy in the marriage. One must always be leery of partners who, to avoid conflict, do not communicate their true thoughts and feelings. Spouses who never get angry or who avoid conflict or who always seem happy are not being real and genuine, and can't contribute to the making of an honest and open marriage.

Good communication in a marriage means there will be a certain amount of appropriate conflict, disagreement, and anger. How can a spouse know what the other spouse's thinking or feeling unless both are honest in communicating? In a marriage where this doesn't happen both partners are at fault—the silent partner who fails to communicate his true thoughts and feelings, and the other partner for living in a dream world of denial and for being insensitive to the fact that something is bothering the other.

Marriages fail because two people fail.

Sometimes conflictual spouses won't separate and they continue in their sadomasochistic relationship. Even when I've recommended divorce or separation for such spouses, they continue living together. They seem to thrive in the conflictual atmosphere. It becomes a way of life. But the conflict is a destructive type of conflict (sometimes including physical violence). The parties become locked into a pattern that only death will stop.

The degree of the depth and breadth of the feelings stirred up by divorce will often be determined by the length of the marriage, the causes of the breakup, and the bitterness and anger that may be involved. There's an emotional jungle that must be traversed. There may be healthy guilt and healthy shame that need to be resolved, and distinguished from unhealthy guilt and unhealthy shame.

Seeking Counseling, Seeking God

Divorced people need counseling as much as they need legal assistance. They need to talk about the marriage breakup. Family and friends are a necessary support system, but they can handle only so much of the emotional fall-out. Usually these caring people are not clinically equipped to help the divorced person sort out what led to the marital breakup. Sometimes well-meaning friends aggravate the post-divorce situation, or they may even be part of the problem! This is why support groups for the divorced and separated are necessary, because the people in them are on the same journey and can walk together toward healing. Participants can understand and

The task of the divorced person is to discover why the marriage failed.

empathize with each other but they can also confront, when necessary.

These support groups are not supposed to provide a setting in which one looks for a new mate. The group should be an oasis in which one finds support, healing, understanding, and the chance to renew oneself. The ministry to the divorced is a modern reenactment of the parable of the Good Samaritan in the sense that the groups pour healing oil on the wounds of those who have been divorced.

Divorced people show two strong tendencies. They are either obsessed with blaming the other partner or they become very negative about themselves, taking on all or too much of the responsibility for the marital failure. The realistic task before the divorced person is to discover how and why the marriage failed. Allied to that, the question must be asked: "How did *I* fail?" Marriages fail because two people fail. The legal, adversarial system tends to distract the divorced from looking at their part in the failed marriage. Counseling gives couples the opportunity to address these questions.

Even in extreme cases, where there has been abuse, the victim must eventually acknowledge their own failure in the relationship. Such an acknowledgment does not in any way condone or excuse abuse. The abused person has to ask why she chose such a person to be her spouse in the first place, and whether she enabled or allowed abusive treatment to persist. Why did she remain in such a destructive relationship? Did abuse occur in her past? The insights gained from these questions are a valuable protection against allowing similar relationships to occur again.

Understanding the dynamics of the former marriage and gaining insight into oneself greatly benefit a divorced person's healing and hope for the future. The person's vision is enriched, as is her understanding of the past and of her future direction. Many divorced people feel bad about themselves and see themselves as failures and as worthless. But the fact that they failed in a marriage doesn't mean that they are failures of life. They can learn, grow, and move on.

If there are any personal weaknesses and unresolved issues from a person's past life, passing through a divorce will surface and magnify them. The divorce will force people to identify these issues and weaknesses, face them, and break through any denial of issues. Whether the divorced persons do this or not will be their choice, and that choice will affect their future relationships. All will depend on the willingness of the divorced person to take responsibility for their part in the failure of the marriage. Becoming stuck in self-deprecation and self-hate can be a means of avoiding any possibility of growth or understanding of the failed marriage. Getting stuck in self-pity and in self-hate causes people to become very self-centered and prevents them from making the necessary changes in their own lives.

Some people go into superficial and emotional liaisons or quick marriages after a divorce. They are extremely needy persons who become destructively dependent and never come to grips with who they are or with what happened to them. Others, who don't work through the painful, emotional event that divorce is, become bitter, enraged, or revengeful. They displace their displeasure on the world around them and blame others for their unhappiness. They are hurting people who refuse to look honestly at themselves and their failed marriage, so they remain incapable of healthy relationships. The divorced can help themselves heal by physical exercise, developing new interests, or diversifying social contacts. Everyone must choose the coping mechanism he or she finds helpful.

For many, the Exodus experience of divorce has brought them to a promised land where they can function healthily again. It has meant becoming a person appreciative of their individuality and of the gift of who they are. Some have found an independence and self-reliance that has enabled them to take responsibility for their lives more than at any other time. All this was done by breaking out of a relationship that was not life-giving. Would some people have changed if it had not been for their divorce?

Forgiveness is a key factor in determining whether a divorced person is healed. The divorced person needs to forgive the former spouse in order to be able to let go of anger, hurt, and all the other painful feelings and memories. Forgiving doesn't mean forgetting. It doesn't mean condoning the former spouse's misbehavior or casually absolving them. It doesn't mean reconciling or taking the person back. That can't be done because trust has been destroyed. It doesn't mean the former spouse has to know about the forgiveness. However, it does mean letting go of all that has been resolved and processed, putting it in God's hands, and moving on. If someone chooses to wallow in hurt and anger he is playing the role of the victim. He is having a pity party.

OTHERS HURT, TOO

We remind ourselves that divorce affects many people and indeed, all society. The most affected people are the children of the broken marriage, for there is also a broken family involved. Parents hesitate to leave a broken marriage because of the effect it will have on the children, while at the same time they are anxious and worried about the effect they are having on the children by remaining in a "bad" marriage. The whole family becomes dysfunctional. This is an agonizing subject for many people contemplating divorce. It haunts them to the degree that they very often delay filing for divorce. "What is the best for the children?" they ask. Counseling can be of some assistance in determining their final decision. There is no easy answer. The problem requires a lot of thought, prayer, discernment, and assistance from wise people.

Parents need to communicate with their children according to their ages, as much as they need to know about the marital situation. This will help alleviate some of the children's anxieties and fears, and will remove any guilt or shame they may have about being the cause of the divorce. They will realize that they are loved and will be taken care of, and that they will be able to see both parents after the divorce.

Children need to be able to talk to their parents about what is happening or at least to some other trusted figure. They need to be able to express their fears, sadness, anger, or other feelings. Parents should never think the children's silence is a sign they are coping with the breakup. In fact, the opposite is more likely: their silence signifies they're avoiding dealing with this painful situation. Sometimes parents want to believe that their children are not bothered by the divorce when instead, the children are full of fear, anxiety, hurt, and anger. At the same time, the children may be afraid to express their feelings, or they may act out those feelings in a rebellious way at home or in school.

Adult children of divorcing parents, whether married or single, also have difficulties when their parents separate after thirty or forty years of marriage.

There is a tendency to disregard the adult children of divorcing parents as if they are immune to what is happening to their parents. On the contrary, they suffer much from their parents' divorce. A late divorce is emotionally disruptive for the adult children and for their own families. They may be old enough to understand what is happening and why, but that's no help. They may feel torn and full of ambivalent feelings toward both parents. The divorce of their parents causes multiple problems, especially during holidays and family celebrations.

Many other issues arise that can affect the adult children in various ways. They will not only start reviewing the family history, but their own lives and relationships as well. Whatever may be the issues, the children will benefit from talking about what exactly happened to their family and to their parents' marriage, while at the same time surfacing all their feelings about the matter.

The good news is that if parents heal from their breakup, eventually their children will also heal and adjust. As the parents heal they will be more able to focus on their children and assist them. This is a phenomenon I have often noticed when counseling divorced parents who are concerned about their children's welfare. Reassuring parents in counseling that, as they heal, their healing will be a benefit to the children, gives parents the hope and support they need and often motivates them to persevere with the counseling process.

Sometimes I have talked with the children of divorced parents because of their own problems or because the parents have requested that I meet with them. For the most part, unless the children have very serious emotional problems, they seem to take their cue from the parents. When parents are stuck in their recovery, so are the children. They may either act out or become very passive. When parents fail to seek help and bungle their lives even further, the consequences are noticeably apparent in the unsettled behavior of the children.

Divorced people are not outcasts from the Christian community.

In these matters we are usually referring to the custodial parent with whom the children live the majority of the time. Most of the time this custodial parent is the mother, and women are often more open to getting counseling than men. I am not indicating that many fathers have not also journeyed on this same road and done a wonderful job, but the majority of custodial parents are women. Very often the father becomes a "sugar daddy" who wines and dines the children and provides them with fun on weekends. He is not a genuine parent anymore. Frequently the men also become involved with another woman and marry quickly, all of which adds to the children's problems.

The mother needs to deal with these new wrinkles which affect her and the children. How she handles her own feelings and what she says about the father will have an impact on the children as to how they will comport themselves with their father. These factors can aggravate and compound her problems with the children, but, again, the better she deals with her own emotional turmoil the more maturely she will be able to cope with what is happening and therefore, be a positive influence on her children. Truthfulness, as difficult as it may be for her and the children, will be the freeing and the healing factor in such a situation.

Many divorced fathers have their own brand of suffering, especially when the angry and frustrated mother uses the children to retaliate against him. Children are caught between their parents, and this aggravates their emotional turmoil. They become a means with which the mother attempts to manipulate, control, and punish the father. This indeed is emotional abuse, not only of the father but of the children as well.

Children will suffer immensely anytime one parent defames the other. There will always be a backlash from the children when this happens, and the defaming parent will lose the respect of the children. They may even be openly hostile or act in a passive-aggressive way to the parent who acts so irresponsibly and immaturely.

Parents can honestly acknowledge certain faults and failings of the other parent when children complain about them. The thing is not to be malicious when speaking about the other parent, but to acknowledge that this is the way mom or dad is. The children can be asked, how do you feel about this behavior? Sometimes children need to be encouraged to speak to the other parent about how they feel and what they think of his unacceptable behavior.

Divorced parents always need to encourage their children to do the best they can in relating to the other parent, no matter how difficult the other parent may be at times. Whether the children succeed or not, at least the encouraging parent can be satisfied that they tried to do the best they could. They will not be obstacles to the children's relationship with the other parent, but they will help the children to deal sensibly with the difficult parent. Children come to the realization that this is their father or mother with all their faults, and they need to do the best they can in relating to him or her in an honest and mature way.

Christians and Divorce

Because of their lingering memories of the Church's past condemnation of divorce, many Catholics still have a difficult time admitting the need for divorce. Christians recall that Scripture says we are not supposed to divorce. Indeed, the Bible and Jesus speak out against divorce, and this only adds to their guilt and shame. But although they did fail in marriage and need to find out the reasons for the failure, but they are not bad people. They are suffering people, like the man in the story of the Good Samaritan, who was wounded and in need of help.

Divorced people are not outcasts from the Christian community. They are not out of the Church, or excommunicated. They can and should receive the Eucharist. They are wounded and hurting people who *need* the Eucharist. If anyone requires this spiritual nourishment, they do! The Eucharist is for people on a journey who are in recovery and struggling with life's issues. Granted this is an immense change in the Church's attitude but it is more in line with the mind of Christ, who is compassionate, merciful, forgiving, and loves all his people.

9.

Loss of a Loved One

The two most important events in our life are birth and death. The birth of a child is celebrated with great joy and exultation. We commemorate that eventful day by celebrating the person's birthday every year. The death of a person we love is met with sadness, but also with a sense of celebration as we recall the person's life. We give thanks to God for who they were. Sometimes we remember to celebrate that person's day of death each year by visiting the burial site or by some religious ceremony. By remembering, we continue our relationship with the loved one.

In the Preface of the Mass of the Resurrection, celebrated for a deceased person, we read, "Life is changed, not ended." As the person's life is changed, so our relationship with our loved one is also changed, not ended. To grieve for our loved ones is to continue our relationship with them. Since grieving is painful, however, people have a tendency to avoid or shorten or quickly terminate their grieving. No relationship with the deceased can be completed or healed unless we grieve. If we loved that person, we need to grieve. Grieving is part of living and of the genuine loving of another person. If we can experience the joys of life, then we can also experience the sadness of life. Life and death are a mixed bag of joy and sadness.

The death of a person we love is one of the most stressful times we have to endure. Like all stress this particular one will only be resolved by facing it and working our way through it. The death of a loved one is a harsh, irreversible reality that forces us to adjust, to adapt, and to change our lives. After a death we do not go back to "business as usual." Someone is gone.

Grieving is a human journey, but also a spiritual one. Faith does not take away our tears. There are no shortcuts through the grieving process. We cannot rationalize, deny, or pretend that the loved one has not died. We cannot minimize loss by the use of pietistic statements that focus strictly on heaven to the exclusion of human pain. We cannot use faith to cover up the reality or the pain of our loss.

John, suddenly a widower, is perplexed because he truly believes his wife is safe with God and that he will see her again some day; so why is he sad and why is he crying? Why does he feel so alone, and so angry about her death? John is experiencing the normal thoughts and feelings of grieving.

As much as we have learned about our human nature through the centuries, we will still have difficulty accepting the deaths of our loved ones. In fact, in the Western world, we probably have regressed in the area of grieving because of our attempts to soften or short-circuit the grieving process.

FUNERAL RITES

It's discouraging to realize that the Western world is becoming less ritualistic, losing its traditions and customs and moving toward briefer funeral rites. At times there is barely any ritual at all. The tendency in the West seems to be: "Get it over with as soon as possible and move on with life." Sometimes this is exemplified by the way the funeral cortege (after the burial) rushes out of the cemetery with breakneck speed. People can't seem to wait to have some food and drink, alcohol included, to soothe their pain and forget the sad, unfortunate reality of loss. The uncomfortable reality of death is toned down, reflected in our attempts to mitigate the harsh but real aspect of death, painful as it is. Doesn't the dignity of the deceased person deserve a significant remembrance? What about the needs of the survivors to have an opportunity to mourn?

Noticeable also today are the less frequent visits people make to cemeteries to pay their respects to the deceased. The upkeep of burial sites is often contracted with the cemetery or neglected altogether. When in Italy some years ago I was impressed to see, on Sunday afternoons, cemeteries crowded with families gathered together with a picnic lunch at the grave of a loved one. It was touching to realize that these people remembered their loved ones who were still part of their lives. The picnic was a family celebration, a reunion. The more we celebrate death, the more we celebrate and appreciate life. When the dead are not given proper respect, respect for life itself is in jeopardy.

Granted, some of those buried in cemeteries lost the respect of family and friends because of their harmful behavior to them, and this deserves recognition. But sometimes a visit to the grave by family, friends, and victims will be a healing experience. The visit affords the survivor an opportunity to heal. They can resolve some of their hurt by an imaginary dialogue with the deceased for their former unacceptable behavior, and by recalling old memories, both sad and joyful.

WAKES

Wakes are psychologically very important for the grieving family. They don't have to be long, but it is necessary that those who grieve see the person they loved for the last time. Viewing of the dead person provides us with the opportunity to face the reality that the person is gone, and therefore, to break through any denial we might be indulging in. It also opens up for us the grieving process. Tears flow, memories come back, stories about the deceased are shared. There is crying and laughter, people hug one another, and the support of friends consoles.

Many feel that large wakes are not necessary. Some complain that wakes become too much like extravaganzas or that a circus atmosphere prevails. We should always aim at what is appropriate and respectful, and treat grieving people as well as the dead person with a sense of their dignity. One way of helping to ensure appropriate and dignified funeral rites and services is to have families gather beforehand and prepare the rites and services.

When we "celebrate" a person's death we tell the story of their lives, the impact they had on our lives whether good or bad. The more we appreciate the gift of life the more we mourn its loss. When we "celebrate" a person's death it doesn't mean that we remove or ignore the painful grieving that lies ahead, but that we gain the strength and confidence to walk the journey through the dark valley of grieving.

Losing a Spouse or a Child

The death of a loving spouse is one of the most stressful periods of a person's life. Adapting to such a loss requires numerous adjustments. We are reminded each day, in multiple and various ways, of our connection with and dependency on the person we have lost. Each day another issue, another problem reminds the surviving spouse that the other person is gone. Life is different. People who are mourning the loss of loved ones need to be reassured that their grieving will last a long time. It takes awhile for some, more time than others, to accept and heal from the death of a loved one. We will always miss the other person. But we make adjustments and we go on.

Parents who have lost children, teenagers, or young adults, never forget the loss of their children. Recovering from such a loss is, for many, a lifelong journey. There are constant reminders that someone is missing. Acceptance of the loss doesn't mean that there are not lifelong consequences and a mixture of memories, but we still try to go on with our lives. These are important considerations, reassuring to people who think there is something wrong with them because of their frequent sad thoughts about and feelings for the loved one who is gone. But something may be wrong if we completely forget the beloved and significant person.

Sometimes, people dealing with such serious loss fall into deep depression and need medication and counseling. Actually, even after their recovery from the depression, sadness will be part of their lives. Yet sadness can be a healthy emotion. It reflects our sense of loss. Counseling will help grieving people get back on track so they can move on with their lives, but memories of the lost loved one will recur from time to time.

Our friends are an important support for us during times of loss. Often, those friends will appear in great numbers to support us and express their condolences, to be present with us, listen to us, cry with us, and share memories and stories of the deceased. Eventually most of these friends will have to get on with their lives. A few will remain to comfort and listen to us. Others see us returning to work and to our daily routine, and sometimes they may think that the family members are "doing well" and seem to have bounced back after the loss of their mother. Yes, it's true—the husband is back to work; the kids are getting on with school, but all concerned may be in much emotional pain as they try to make daily adjustments for the absence of a mother and wife.

Sometimes friends who were initially very supportive become uncomfortable if those grieving continue to openly express their grief and need to talk about the deceased. Sometimes these friends begin to back away from us. Others may make inappropriate statements: "Pull yourself together. You need to get on with your life. You have grieved enough. The children need you to be strong. You need to get out and start dating." Such people mean well, but they are totally insensitive to the grieving person's state of mind and feelings. Such friends usually have erroneous ideas about grieving and so are not prepared to respond appropriately to a grieving person.

Often a grieving person may begin to think something is wrong with him or her because they are still grieving the death of a loved one months later. Rather, something is wrong with those who do not allow the grieving person to grieve fully and completely. These people mean well, but they don't understand grieving. They may find it difficult to handle their own feelings, and so do not know how to listen and empathize with the pain of others. The death of a loved one is a common denominator for all of us. It is a normal but painful aspect of life. Frequently counseling is necessary when people are not handling daily life, and when people are depressed because they are not working through their feelings, have minimized them, or are not in touch with them.

I remember sharing with a friend the deep sadness and hurt I was feeling over the loss of another very close friend. I was met with silence, and left hanging. Sometimes, people you share your grief with are emotionally immobilized and make no response. They are in shock. They appear insensitive, but are really at a loss as to how to act or what to say, so they retreat into silence. However true this may be, in my case, my friend's silence left me hurt, angry, and disappointed at his insensitivity. I was more cautious afterwards about whom I shared my loss with. If people don't know how to grieve, they can't relate to others who are grieving.

Friends often don't realize that grieving over lost loved ones may last a long time. When grieving people realize that their support system is disappearing they begin to go underground with their pain. That is, permission to grieve publicly has been removed, so they keep their grief within themselves or cautiously speak to someone whom they trust. Some will seek out a bereavement group or grief counseling, where their grieving is accepted. Bereavement groups in our churches are probably the most important services any community can provide. Bereavement groups give people permission to grieve. We need to constantly reassure others that their grieving is OK.

Facing the reality of the death of a loved one is a constant acknowledgment that they are gone, especially in the case of sudden and unexpected deaths. In our waking moments in the morning and at times during the day the reality of loss strikes us again and again, "like a thief in the night." The acknowledgment of this harsh reality is difficult, but it keeps us mentally and spiritually sound and on the road to healthy grieving. This acknowledgment breaks through any denial and any pretending that may have entered our grieving process. As God calls us to face our loss he also walks with us, so that we realize more and more that grieving is a spiritual journey. We come to know ourselves, the deceased, and God much better. Yes, we are brought together with others; but, in time, we will be alone, face to face with God—a moment of spiritual intimacy.

HEALTHY GRIEVING

Healthy grieving is emotionally expressive, and assists us to move through the sadness and the other feelings that accompany grief. Sadness is a good emotion; it reflects our love for and attachment to the person who has died. Various levels and degrees of sadness can last a long time, but people can function, can go on with their daily lives, even when they are sad. They don't become helpless or hopeless.

When people get stuck in grieving and can't move on they are often trapped in anger. This anger may be hidden or unrecognized. Time and effort may be needed to resolve this anger. It may mean talking with others or seeking professional help. People also need to examine their thinking patterns and belief system, which may be negative or neurotic: "I can't live without my wife." "I'll never be anything without him." "I can't go on alone." "God is punishing me." These and other negative thoughts need to be avoided, or they will engender more hurt and more anger and keep on refueling painful, difficult feelings. Negative and erroneous beliefs can be challenged and changed, but feelings may take a longer time to heal. Correct thinking helps us to heal wounded feelings instead of aggravating them.

Grieving people are often amazed at how many unresolved issues and forgotten memories surface at the death of a loved one. Some of these memories may be related in one way or another to the deceased, but others may have no connection with the dead person. Grieving has a way of surfacing the many painful and broken aspects of our lives, even aspects we had thought were neatly packed away. Grieving can also remind us of happy, joyful occasions and the many aspects of our relationship with the dead person, aspects that evoke gratitude and satisfaction.

Grieving is a feeling process, so we need to give ourselves permission to feel any emotion, and not allow unhealthy guilt or shame to prevent us from feelings. These feelings are difficult and painful, but processing them will eventually heal them. This is what John Gray tells us in his excellent book *If We Can Feel It, We Can Heal It*. What often occurs at the death of a loved one is that people bury not only the body but their feelings. If this happens, grieving is never resolved because the feelings connected with it have been buried. These unresolved feelings may be manifested in numerous destructive ways—physically, emotionally, and spiritually. Relationships will suffer, too. Burial is not the end of grieving; it's only the beginning.

Healthy grieving is emotionally expressive.

There's a difference between sadness and depression. Sadness is feeling the pain of loss. Someone we loved is gone, but we are still functioning and carrying on with our daily lives. Depression involves being overwhelmed by our loss, becoming helpless, being unable to function, and without hope. And all these feelings are buried, especially anger. The survivor is numb, and may even develop physical illnesses. Frequently, grieving people's depression is aggravated by the existence of unresolved issues in their lives as well as by unresolved conflicts with the deceased person, conflicts that need to be addressed even now.

Often we hear people ask, "How did those parents handle the death of their teenage daughter?" And the response we may hear is: "They were really strong. They didn't shed a tear. Remember you have to be strong for the children." Translated, this means: "Don't cry or show any painful emotions." Or we may hear well-meaning people say, "Don't cry. They're better off now that they're with God." This is a pseudo-spiritual statement to block grieving. Such statements run contrary to the meaning of grieving and the human condition.

Funeral homes can be the site of insensitive remarks. I've even heard clergy delivering all sorts of spiritual clichés and bromides to a grieving family, but not one crumb of ordinary human compassion and feeling dropped from their lips. The grieving family feels grateful about the clergyman's visit, but I'm sure his irrelevant and impersonal statements did not help them feel their grief.

Hiding Grief

People who hide their grief are not showing strength, but weakness

The emotionally strong allow themselves to feel and express their feelings.

or a fear of suffering. They are afraid of difficult and uncomfortable feelings. They are afraid they are going to fall apart and feel ashamed. Yet grieving is partly about allowing ourselves to feel uncomfortable. Sometimes we hear statements of denial and avoidance with regard to grieving. "Dad wouldn't want us to cry, but to be happy and remember the good times." And what about the eulogist who delivers one joke and humorous story after another about the deceased in order to divert his listeners—and himself—from feeling the pain of loss.

Jesus leaves us with a beautiful, but powerful example of what it means to be human and spiritual. John writes of Jesus' reacting to the death of his friend Lazarus, "Jesus wept" (John 11:35). William Barclay in his commentary on this text says "We are shown the picture of Jesus wrung with anguish as he shared the anguish of the human heart."

The emotionally strong allow themselves to feel and express their feelings. Our feelings of guilt, anger, and regret may not always be logical, but they are our feelings. They are not bad. We need to own and feel them and understand them. These feelings may be rooted in experiences of the past or they may be emanating from negative thinking, which we need to correct. Think of parents who are furious with a doctor whom they claim misdiagnosed their child's illness and, as a result, the child died. Perhaps other parents are angry with God, believing that God is punishing them for a previous abortion, or the daughter who feels guilty because she wasn't present, through no fault of her own, when her mother died. She also regrets she didn't do more for her mother when she was alive, which may be true or not. These are the many thoughts and feelings that grieving requires us to experience, explore, and explain to ourselves and others. Permission to feel means also to be able to feel anger toward God, the person who died, and toward whomever else we need to be angry with.

The death of a loved one leaves us with many loose ends: bills unpaid, accumulated debts, business ventures never completed or mishandled, plans and goals unfulfilled. All these issues can deepen and aggravate our grieving. More difficult to face are the unresolved issues and conflicts in a relationship. These make the grieving process even more complicated. The hurts, anger, and disappointments we experienced with the deceased remain with us and still require our attention. But the dead are the easiest people with whom we have to deal and to relate. They don't have any more problems with us. They see everything clearly. They hold no grudges and are quite agreeable. We can resolve everything with them; we can say whatever we wish to them and express all our feelings about them, especially our anger.

I often recommend that grieving people go to the cemetery and talk to and argue with deceased loved ones. Let it all hang out! The dead won't become defensive! We may not have been able or willing to communicate with the dead in life, but in death we can, especially when it comes to difficult parents or other people with whom we may have had irreconcilable differences. We need to do this for ourselves. It is all part of the grieving process. At times it helps to write a letter to the deceased person. Talking to the dead in a place meaningful to you and the deceased can also help. It is my experience that grieving people can resolve their hurts and anger in these ways more quickly and more easily than they could while the deceased was alive.

Our relationship with the deceased loved one is changed, not ended. We can ask for their help and ask for their prayers. They can be a big support to us in death—sometimes much more so than they were in life.

THE RIPPLE EFFECT

Sometimes grieving is compounded by a ripple effect—other losses that are the consequences of and are connected with the loved person's death. Loss of a spouse can mean the loss of financial aid, companionship, sexual and emotional intimacy, the loss of future opportunities and possibilities, the hopes and dreams never to be fulfilled. There are retirement plans, vacations, and trips together that will never happen. People who are grieving may have a difficult time admitting these ripple effects, sometimes out of a sense of shame or from thinking they should not be feeling that way. Sometimes they are afraid of being angry with the dead. This is all part of grieving. Each loss must be recognized and the feelings and regrets connected with it experienced.

Grieving can be compounded as when a woman's husband of thirty years dies and her mother is, at the same time, dying of cancer. The widow is about to lose her job. The car she is driving has a dead battery, and her son is failing courses in his senior year of college. One loss after another magnifies the original loss of her husband, with whom she becomes more angry and frustrated because he didn't take better care of his health. Here she is alone, without his help, and she is angry with him. She laments: "Will I ever get through all this?" Yes, she will if she wants to heal, but it will take time and much grieving.

She will have to take life one day at a time and deal with one loss at a time, preferably the loss that is more important on a particular day. She will need to discover what loss she needs to grieve for most. Often when a woman is overwhelmed with losses, the major loss, her husband's death, can be sidelined. There are so many immediate losses that need to be addressed. Many of these immediate losses can sometimes be intensified because her husband isn't there to help her. Grieving is not necessarily a nice, neat package, but whenever it surfaces it needs to be addressed.

The sudden death of a father who was in good health leaves the family in a state of shock and turmoil. They have to make funeral arrangements quickly. They swing between disbelief and emotional upheavals, between crying and laughing, between being nervous and feeling numb. Amidst all the post-funeral activities and confusion the serious journey of grieving may not take place for days or weeks or even months, until the shocking reality of a loved one's death sets in. But grieving will eventually begin, unless people bury their emotions in order to get on with their lives.

The death of a mother who has been terminally ill and died by inches leaves the family in a state of grieving over a long period of time. By the time the mother dies the family is prepared to some degree for her death. They have already been grieving but there is still that final, awesome reality: she is now gone. They will never see her again on this earth. The long journey of caring for her has been completed. She is dead.

While this type of death takes its toll on loved ones, they have already been grieving over their inevitable loss. They may feel an uncomfortable ambivalence—sadness at the loss of their mother, but relief that she is suffering no more. They feel relief that their long, tiring vigil is over. They are able to go back to the former routines of their lives. Such feelings of relief are normal. There is no reason to give in to feelings of unhealthy guilt or shame, no need to feel that one is disloyal because of this feeling of relief.

Decisions

If at all possible, grieving people need to avoid making major decisions too soon after the death of a loved one, especially in the early days of grieving. Too often such decisions are not based on reason, but on impulse during the painful turmoil of grieving. For example, an elderly woman sells her house a month after her husband's death and moves in with her daughter's family. The children's concern for their mother living alone makes them put pressure on her to move in. Whether or not this is the best decision for the mother and her daughter will take some time to resolve and involve lengthy discussion with the family. Moving too fast and acting impulsively or out of anxiety frequently mean wrong decisions are being made.

We also see grieving husbands remarrying within a year, or even months, after the death of their wives, because they are not able to live alone. Frequently, in such premature second marriages, the husband's way of dealing with grief is an escape from the pain of loss. Such second marriages often prove troublesome. The man may eventually become depressed, physically ill, or have sexual problems in his second marriage. He was not ready for remarriage because he had not completed or even begun grieving for his deceased wife.

If there are children from the previous marriage they may feel hurt, or feel resentful toward their father, especially if they are adult children. Since they are still in the throes of grieving over their mother's death, they find their father's behavior insensitive to them and disloyal to their mother. They may resent and even be hostile to the father's new wife. The children probably don't realize that their father is handling his grief by escaping into marriage. Eventually the children will feel a double loss: the death of their mother and the loss, to another woman, of their father. Often the family will be torn apart by the father's behavior.

When a widow or widower who is suffering from loneliness or looking for someone to take care of them physically and emotionally gets married, soon after the death of the spouse, we have to question the advisability of such a marriage. In all such cases, people need to move cautiously, to get advice from others, or, possibly seek counseling.

DIFFERENT WAYS OF GRIEVING

People do grieve in different ways, but some ways are healthy and some are not. Some grieve immediately and move smoothly through the process. Others have a delayed reaction that may appear later on in the form of depression or some other form of illness. Delayed grieving may even be triggered off months after a funeral by some event connected with the deceased or a forgotten memory. One truth remains: we can't avoid grieving. It's always there until we face it, move through it, and resolve it.

As members of a family relate in life, so they will relate at the death of a family member. If silence is their pattern of relating then their grief will be faced in the same way—with silence. If the family is conflictual, then the death of the parent will surface unresolved conflicts and disputes, together with the resultant anger. The terms of a will (often) provide an area for conflicts, claims of unfairness, and blaming. In fact, sometimes disputes over the parents' material goods are ways in which people are distracted from focusing on the real issue of grieving. Some families are experts at dealing with family issues on an intellectual basis but without the interjection of any of their feelings. If so, this is also the way they will deal with the death of a family member: "Mother is now at peace and happy with the Lord. So let us eat, drink, and be merry, for tomorrow we die."

Dysfunctional families will deal with their grief in dysfunctional ways, which often means not really dealing with it. Some members of such families may wisely seek counseling as a means of finally dealing with the unresolved family issues triggered by a parent's death. Sometimes the death of a parent can be a grace that brings the family together and heals them. Or it can be the occasion when the family splits further apart and family members go their separate ways, which only adds more loss to the loss of a parent. Death in families, especially the death of a parent, has a tremendous amount of meaning and a power all its own. How often one of the married children gets divorced after the death of the parent. Death frequently surfaces many of the weaknesses of the family, including unresolved problems.

RECONCILIATION

When loved ones who have hurt us are dying, the dying period may be a time for reconciliation. It may be that we have offended the dying person and need to make amends—something we probably need to do more for ourselves than for the dying person.

The period of dying can be a grace-filled moment, when barriers between people can be broken down. Understanding and compassion become easier, and forgiveness and reconciliation are possible in the last hours of the dying person. Disagreements that seemed monumental in the past suddenly seem insignificant in the presence of death. Here is an example: Joan has been estranged from her older brother, Tom, who is now dying. She decides to visit her brother. They have not spoken to each other since their mother's death ten years before because of some disagreement over their mother's will, and Joan believed Tom was unfair to her. Joan discusses the matter with the dying Tom, forgives him, and is reconciled with him.

Sometimes broken relationships can be healed only after the death of one of the parties when we realize that the dead people have no more problems. They see everything clearly. Often in the case of a sexually abused person, the abused person feels safer now that the abuser is dead, like the daughter who was sexually abused by her father and can forgive him only after his death.

Often a new level of emotional intimacy springs up between a loved one and a dying person. The wife who cares for her terminally ill husband for months may experience an emotional closeness to him that she never experienced in their thirty years of marriage. The husband, finally, in his physically and emotionally weakened condition, is able to let down his guard and express his loving, tender emotions for his wife. Much can be accomplished when people are dying. It can become a highly emotional time of sharing on a deeper and more profound level never experienced before.

There is probably no more beautiful picture of an intimate relationship as when spouses are walking together in their final days, when one spouse is dying and the other one is there to comfort, console, and care as both continue to live out their vows to be together "in good times and in bad, in sickness and in health, until death do us part." This is a beautiful conclusion to an intimate journey together on this earth.

Our Own Mortality

An aspect of grieving that may often not be expressed, is that the death of a significant person, especially a contemporary, often triggers thoughts and feelings about our own inevitable death. We come face to face with our own mortality in the person who is dying. We can often suppress or avoid thinking about the subject as it may be, yet we need to allow these thoughts and feelings to surface. It is a time to appreciate the gift of life, to take care of that life. It is a time when we can be motivated to make changes in our lives; it can be a time of conversion. It is a time when we can turn back to God or strengthen our relationship with God.

As I write these words, a good friend of mine is dying of an aggressive kind of cancer. It appeared suddenly. Doctors gave him six months to live, and now it's been changed to just a few weeks. I go in and out of disbelief, and am filled with sadness and other feelings that I am trying to deal with. Since he is a contemporary of mine, his dying has an even greater impact on me as I confront my own mortality. How fleeting and fragile life is! I am facing my own anxieties about death as I grieve for Father Joe. I have so many feelings, so many questions and faith issues at a time like this. But I know that the better we grieve over the loss of our loved ones and friends the better we will be prepared for our own death, the final loss.

Gradually, after a period of time, grieving people move to a sense of acceptance and resolution. There is a sense of closure and a letting go. We will always miss the deceased and carry with us memories of him through life. In a certain sense we are healed, but the scars remain. Someone is missing. Life is changed and will never be the same. Holidays and other celebrations will remind us that the loved one is no longer present. We remember the person's birthday and the day of death, significant events in that person's history. In a certain sense we are always in recovery and grieving for the beloved, but we go on.

How much time should elapse before one thinks of remarrying after the death of a spouse? This will differ with each person, but three to five years seems to be an appropriate amount of time. Usually during that same time the children of the first marriage also will have healed. Their healing will usually keep pace with the healing of the living parent. When the living parent is seriously considering remarriage, communication with the children about this is well-advised.

As the years pass, people will shed a tear over or share a sad feeling about a dead person on different occasions, as memories of the deceased surface. This is normal. It certainly doesn't mean we have not grieved properly. If we loved the dead person as an integral part of our lives for many years, we will always remember the person. Life for the deceased is changed, not ended; too, our relationship with the deceased is not ended, but changed. A suggested practice is to light a candle in memory of the loved one when special family meals are shared. It is a loving and consoling remembrance of their invisible presence among us.

If people have repressed their grief, then certain occasions may bring long-repressed feelings to the surface. I've counseled many people who were attending the funeral of a casual friend and who were suddenly overwhelmed with a grief disproportionate to their relationship with the deceased person. But this particular funeral was a moment of grace or a catalyst when their repressed feelings of grief for other close persons, whom they had not grieved for properly, surfaced. Other people will say that they grieved over lost loved ones in their families, only to find out years later that they had grieved with their head but not with their heart. Such grief may not always be recognized, but, when it is, we need the help of insightful people who can help us identify the signs of unresolved grief, and we need the courage to face that grief.

DEALING WITH THE BEREAVED

What about those of us who are present when people are in deep grief—what can we say or do? This is a troubling and anxious time as we approach grieving people whose tears and wounds are exposed.

Actually, there is not much we *can* say or do, except to be present to the bereaved. We can be a sacrament of real presence, when we listen to and allow hurting people to say and feel anything they want to say or feel. Our presence will give them permission to wait and grieve, to laugh and cry, to curse, plead, be angry, or be loving. We need to listen, to be in touch with and comfortable with what they are feeling. There are no magic words, no responses we can make that will bring the deceased person back. Maybe later on we will be able to speak calmly and reasonably with the grieving person and with expressions of consolation and comfort. Now it is enough that we are present, warm and embracing. Our feelings and our faith are what they need. We need to give them space and all the time they need to grieve. In this way we pour the oil and wine of comfort and solace on their wounds.

As the days and weeks go on we should continue to connect with them with visits, phone calls, an occasional note, or whatever it takes to reach out to them and let them know we are there for them, that we care. We must never underestimate the compassionate power of our being present to those who grieve—when we visit them, or when we attend wakes, funeral services, and burials. Our very presence is a healing power.

Death is an ever-present aspect of life, and, after a person's birth, it is the most important event in a person's life. Grieving, therefore, is an essential part of life. We become more human and more Christian the more we grieve. Grieving forces us to grow in faith and hope. It challenges us to look to the life beyond. That is why it is not only a human journey filled with emotion, but a spiritual journey. It is evidence again that all spirituality is rooted in our ability to feel, to be immersed in all aspects of the human condition, the condition in which we find God. Isn't this the story of the incarnation, where Jesus became one like us? Where else in life, but in grieving, are we brought to the depths of our humanness, moved by the deepest emotions, and brought face to face with the meaning of life?

Postscript

While I was writing this chapter, my mother, Viola, then ninety-eight years old, weakened after suffering from congestive heart failure. She had to be placed in a nursing-care facility and needed continual oxygen. I gradually came to accept, with much difficulty, the inevitability of her approaching death. With this realization, the family and I started preparing for her death and for saying our goodbyes. My mother also was aware that her death was near, and she was prepared to leave.

When she died about a month after being placed in the nursing facility, I began to experience what I had been writing about grief. As much as I have grieved over the loss of other loved ones, grieved with others, and comforted and consoled those who are grieving, now it was my time to grieve for someone special, my mother.

Many people responded to my mother's death with kindness, compassion, and caring. I was deeply touched, and could feel the consolation of God coming from them. I will never forget their presence in my life at my time of loss. Even though friends and loved ones participated with me on this journey, there is still the personal part of grieving, those times when I need to talk with my mother about her past life, with all its joys and sorrows. She is still present to me; she helps and comforts me.

There are no shortcuts through grieving. The only course of action is in the counsel I give to others: "Face and walk straight through the journey of grieving."

10.

Anxiety & Fear

Anxiety and fear are aspects of living. If we are alive we experience them. If we deny that we feel anxiety or fear we're not being truthful. The only people without fear and anxiety are dead people, and that's why we can say truthfully about them, "May they rest in peace."

Fear and anxiety are not the same. Fear is a painful feeling of alarm about some trouble we believe is about to befall us. Anxiety is lingering, painful feelings of anguish gnawing at us over some impending or anticipated ill, real or imagined. For all practical purposes, however, popular parlance uses fear and anxiety interchangeably, as we will in this chapter.

Before we delve into the problematic aspects of fear and anxiety, I think it is worthwhile to say that not all fear and anxiety involve a negative experience; they can have positive meaning, too. What causes fear and anxiety to be either negative or positive depends on how we use them, on how we allow them to affect our lives, or on how we may perceive them.

Fear and anxiety can be our friends. They can warn us of impending dangers, and so help us to be alert, guarded, cautious, and to take appropriate means to protect ourselves physically, emotionally, financially, and so on from being harmed. Fear and anxiety provide energy that can be used positively to preserve what we possess, and to protect ourselves. They can prompt us to take positive action and not be passive in the face of trouble.

Often fear and anxiety cause a physical or psychological reaction in us. We tighten up. Our adrenaline flows. We become focused. We begin to think clearly. We are ready to either fight or confront the danger at hand or, if need be, take flight and move away.

The speaker who is about ready to ascend the podium and face a large crowd will often feel anxiety. This anxiety can be used to energize the speaker to be animated, motivated, confident, and convinced of the worth of his presentation. The driver following a weaving, drunken driver uses his anxiety to be alert and to avoid that particular car at all costs by either passing it or dropping back or by turning off in another direction. The person who is accosted by an unhappy and aggressive co-worker may choose to use anxiety to help her speak up and be assertive with the aggressive person, or politely excuse herself, and walk away. In these cases anxiety and fear are used as protective and helpful stimulants to address threatening situations. The emotions energize us so fear and anxiety may be utilized in a constructive way. They can increase a person's confidence so that she thinks clearly and acts effectively and quickly.

Anxiety and fear become negative when they are destructive to our relationship with ourself and with others. When such feelings become so overwhelming that they control our behavior and our thinking, our reasoning can become distorted and we may make poor or wrong decisions. We may act tentatively or impulsively, or not at all; we become passive or paralyzed. We decide to do nothing when action is called for.

When anxiety overtakes us it causes us to lose confidence in ourselves and in our judgment. We begin to feel low self-esteem and guilty when we should not be feeling guilty, or feel shame that some-

It is common for people not to recognize their fear and anxiety.

thing is wrong with us when there isn't. We feel doubt about our ability to do ordinary tasks that previously we have been doing quite well. Sometimes we will act irresponsibly by avoiding a task because of our fear of failure or of what others may think. Or we may do a task poorly because of our nervousness, or over-compensate by putting more energy and time than is necessary into a task. We may lapse into perfectionism because we doubt ourselves and fear that we will make a mistake in doing a task. Perfectionists often procrastinate because they are paralyzed by fear—and then they feel powerless because of their fear of failure.

It is common for people not to recognize their fear and anxiety. They may deny their feelings, repress them, or be out of touch with them. The feelings may appear in physical problems such as heightened blood pressure, blurred vision, headaches, tiredness, difficulty in swallowing or breathing, stomach cramps, or stiffness in one's limbs. We call these ailments psychosomatic, for, although they involve real pain and physical symptoms, they are really caused by the person's anxieties. Other people believe they have all sorts of imaginary illnesses; such people are considered hypochondriacs. These people have internalized their fear and anxiety, which they either do not recognize or do not want to address.

Other people manifest their anxieties by compulsive behavior, repeating the same act and words over and over again. Others may suffer from obsessive thinking, which involves thoughts that continually preoccupy their minds. Sometimes these obsessive thoughts have a religious component—as when the person becomes obsessed with sin where there is no sin, or with being a sinful person. We call this tormenting illness scrupulosity. Still others have a generalized anxiety and nervousness and worry about everything and anything, whether it occurred in the past, is presently happening, or may take place in the future. Sometimes people's anxiety becomes so severe they have panic attacks where they experience trouble breathing, become dizzy, or feel faint.

We all know people who are phobic, which is an all-consuming, morbid anxiety about a particular thing or action. They may be excessively afraid of elevators, or heights, or birds, and so on. But phobias are not the problem; they are symptoms of deep unresolved traumas from past experiences. Phobic people have not processed the pain, the hurt, the anger, and the fears that they experienced at some tragic time in their lives—rather, they have repressed them. Some people suffering from deep depression, high anxiety, and other psychological problems are often victims of post-traumatic stress disorder. They have not addressed and resolved some past trauma that now begins to manifest itself graphically, both physically and emotionally. In fact, many people who are continually anxious have unresolved issues from their past. They need to delve into their lives and deal with the untreated fears, anger, hurts, abuse, losses, and trauma that still plague them. People need to understand their anxieties and fears and get beneath them, face them, and defuse them in order to be freed from their destructive control.

Anxious people not only lack confidence in themselves but can often be mistrustful of others. Sometimes anxiety and depression are so severe that people manifest the signs of paranoia, or they suffer from delusions and hallucinations. Also, when people worry excessively about their physical illnesses, their anxiety aggravates these illnesses. Besides physical ailments, doctors need to treat the illnesses of anxiety and depression, which they often neglect. Only then can a doctor bring complete healing to a patient.

In situations like the above counseling may be necessary, and medication may also be required. Medications will treat the chemical imbalance that has occurred in the brain because of the enormous stress the anxiety has caused. In such situations anxiety, like depression, is an illness, and is treatable with the efficient and sophisticated medications we have today. As we treat the body's illnesses with medication in order to bring about healing, so today we realize that we can treat illnesses of the brain, such as severe anxiety and depression, with effective medication. This is good news. The bad news is that so many people, even the well-educated, suffer from misunderstanding and ignorance about such medications.

Anxiety can also be manifested by negative thinking. Negative thinking fuels anxious feelings, and anxious feelings reinforce negative thinking. It is a vicious cycle. People need to break the cycle first, by changing their negative thinking. I often tell people, before they leave my office, that they can change their negative thinking right there and then, but anxious feelings will take a long time to disappear.

People need to continually repeat to themselves positive and truthful statements until such positive thinking is in charge. For example, "I can speak up to this annoying person." "I will drive over this high bridge." "I am a capable person and I will succeed in my new job." These and many other positive statements need to be expressed repeatedly to ourselves throughout the day even if we don't *feel* positive. Eventually we *will* feel positive about ourselves. Speaking in such a manner is not being hypocritical but truthful with ourselves.

Anxious feelings never disappear completely, but they don't have to be a destructive and controlling aspect of our lives. They can be lessened. We all have anxieties, but we can learn how to deal with them so they don't control our lives. As we build up confidence in ourselves, this confidence will counteract negative thinking.

ANXIETY IN RELATIONSHIPS

Anxiety and fears affect our relationships with others, especially our close relationships. We are at times so taken up with our own fears and anxieties that we don't even realize how self-centered we've become. We can hardly focus on the concerns of others, and we become insensitive to their needs, anxieties, and hurts. We don't listen to what they are saying or look at what may be going on in their lives. We become emotionally distant from the people around us. The other person then feels neglected and unloved, and they understandably become angry and feel hurt. The relationship becomes a one-way street because the person overwhelmed with fears is oblivious to the world and the people around him.

Some spouses feel so anxious about whether they are loved by the other spouse that they either become submissive to the other or obsessed with pleasing the other. They're ready to agree to anything and to do what the other spouse wants in order to be accepted and loved. Or the opposite may be true: one person may be so anxious about being loved by the other that he attempts to be controlling and demanding. Such control has nothing to do with being strong or loving but is another form of insecurity.

Anxiety can be manifested by negative thinking.

Anxiety can also be infectious. The anxieties of the one spouse can cause the other spouse to eventually become full of anxieties. Or the opposite may occur: one spouse becomes distant, uncaring, and insensitive in order to protect himself from being overwhelmed by all the anxieties of the other spouse.

A spouse who is feeling overwhelmed by the other spouse's anxieties may also feel a sense of helplessness and inadequacy in assisting the other. A man often thinks he needs to fix something in his wife and, when he can't, he feels inadequate. Because she doesn't feel assistance and sensitivity from him, she may project anger, resentment, and emotional and sexual distance from him. All this can make the husband feel guilty and shameful about himself, and convinced he is an inadequate husband.

The husband needs to make a leap of faith in himself in spite of his wife's anxieties, or else he will be swallowed up by them. He needs to address his wife's anxieties without being infected by them, to take responsibility for himself and move beyond his own anxieties and guilt to do what he can to improve the marriage. He can do this by being more confident in himself, more present to her, more supportive of her, and more sensitive to her. Confrontation and compassion are both equally important in a loving relationship because they both help express sensitivity and concern.

Anxiety takes many forms in a relationship. They may be about the couple's relationship, or about sexual difficulties, or about problems with the children, or financial concerns, health issues, care of aging parents, or about other stresses that affect families today. Open and honest sharing about these distressing anxieties and fears will strengthen a couple's trust in one another.

Anxiety is frequently the cause of sexual problems in marriage. Our understanding of sexuality and sexual relations has been broadened by new research, and by more sophisticated information than we ever had before. Such information has not only improved marital sexual relations but has eliminated much ignorance and misunderstanding about them. The medical world has developed new and effective medications that not only treat sexual dysfunction but also enhance sexual performance. In spite of all of these wonderful advances, anxiety can still play a major role in marital sexual relations. Such anxiety needs to be addressed by the spouses together, whether the anxiety exists in one or both spouses. Each needs to be sensitive to and understanding of the other.

Anxiety in a marriage may reflect buried resentments toward the other spouse—or even a parent. There may be unresolved hurts, anger, abuse, or traumas from the past. Sexual ignorance, fear of pregnancy, feelings of inadequacy, low self-esteem, guilt, shame, and a score of other psychological problems also can be the source of anxiety in a marriage. Unrealistic expectations about one's sexual performance, the size of one's genitals or breasts, or about one's body image can all create anxiety which will, in turn, sabotage sexual functioning and satisfaction. Such anxiety can be resolved, but only if it is addressed. Our sexuality is an integral and sensitive part of our personhood. Because it is so delicate even the least amount of anxiety can disturb our sexual tranquility.

In any important relationship people need to recognize their anxiety about the issues and the problems they may be having. They need to talk about these fears and anxieties, listen to each other's description of anxieties, and share their feelings about them. This will help them to manage and regulate their anxieties, keep them from getting out of control, and help move through them. Thus, they can utilize the energy of anxiety in a constructive manner, rather than in a destructive way, which only paralyzes the couple and compounds their problems.

Ways to Cope

There are several steps that can help us deal with our fears and anxieties.

1. *Awareness.* It is important that we be aware of the times we are feeling fear and anxiety in ourselves, in our bodies, in our thinking. Denial, pretension, acting with false bravado, blaming others, or

minimizing the presence of anxieties does not make them go away. They will only be manifested in tension, stress, irritability, or they may cause physical problems.

2. *Acceptance.* Realizing we have fears and anxieties makes us realistic, and then we can do something about them. Therefore, we need to accept our fears and anxieties, realizing that they are and will be part of our life. Let's not be surprised at their presence. Even Jesus had to deal with fears and anxieties.

3. *Address our anxieties.* We do this by talking about them with someone, so as to put them in perspective. We should discuss all the feelings connected with our anxieties so that we can defuse them and weaken their power over us. If I fear the lump I have on my shoulder, just worrying about it will only make me feel more anxious; I must seek medical attention. It may be nothing or it may be serious, but it can be treated. Whatever the fear may be, feel it—and do whatever you need to do. As Susan Jeffers says in her book *Feel the Fear and Do It Anyway:*

The disciples of Jesus were hiding behind locked doors out of fear. Jesus goes through these locked doors. We need to "go through" our fears, and not let them lock us out from life. We need to face the people and situations we fear. We will feel more confident and better about ourselves after we do this. We become strengthened and assertive. We need to speak up for ourselves, or else we will allow others to control our lives through our fears. We will always feel better about ourselves even if we don't win the argument or convince another. We will have a better respect for ourselves, and so will others.

4. *Analyze our fears and anxieties.* Where did they come from? Did we learn to be anxious from living with anxious parents in an anxious home? Perhaps we were not loved, caressed, affirmed, or cared for. Perhaps we were put down, neglected, or excessively criticized. Did we suffer trauma, tragedies, or abuse? Whatever may have been the cause of anxiety needs to be surfaced, dealt with, and talked about.

Counseling can be of great assistance in helping us to surface and resolve those painful aspects of the past that are generating so much of our anxiety. Sometimes medication will be necessary because we have inherited a chemical imbalance from one or both of our parents. Other times, the overwhelming stresses of life cause not only

> *Minimizing the presence of anxieties does not make them go away.*

anxieties, but because of an excessive amount of stress, a chemical imbalance in the brain. We can help ourselves not only by getting counseling, but also with effective, prescribed medication. There is help. There is no need to pass these illnesses on from generation to generation, we can move beyond our past.

One thing is certain: we will have to learn how to recognize and live with anxieties, get beyond them, and not let them control our lives. Jesus said something to this effect when he said, "If anyone comes to me without setting aside his mother and father, wife and children, brothers and sisters, and even his own life, he cannot be my disciple" (Luke 14:26). He is calling us to move beyond our past. We do not blame our parents. They did the best they knew how. They didn't have the information and skills we have available to us today.

5. *Live in the present moment.* This is one of the soundest ways to keep our anxieties in check.

6. *Alleviate anxieties.* We can do this by letting go of them. When we have accepted and addressed our fears and anxieties we can't let them linger inside of ourselves, or else they will become destructive of us and our relationships. We need to let go and move on and trust in ourselves.

"Yesterday is past. Tomorrow isn't here. Today is the present and that's why we call it a gift." So many people multiply and compound their anxieties by living in the past with all its regrets, self-doubt, guilt, and questionable decisions, with things they think they should have done or not have done—all the "what ifs" and possibilities they have never addressed. They continue to carry these anxieties throughout life, and this not only infects their lives with nervousness and worrying but also complicates their lives.

Tomorrow isn't here, but some people worry about what will or will not happen tomorrow. Their worry is not just a normal preparation for tomorrow's events, but an obsession with avoiding any possible mistakes. They will compulsively think and talk about tomorrow, next week, or next year. They anticipate the worse. Their thinking becomes an endless series of "what ifs." Their fears and anxieties increase, draining away their self-confidence and energy, disrupting their reasoning power and judgment, and setting them up for possible mistakes because they are so tense.

Apprehension about tomorrow's events can cause confusion, uptightness, irritability, and a poor perception of reality. Situations are always magnified and made to look worse than they are. Studies show that almost eighty percent of what we worry about never happens, and when it does happen, it usually doesn't occur in the way it was imagined. Also, unrealistic expectations set people up for even more fears and anxieties and disappointments.

A focus on the present helps us not only to thank God for this day, but to realize that God's will is before us in what we have to do, such as getting the children off to school, dealing with issues at work, cooperating with difficult people, and keeping our appointment with the doctor. We motivate ourselves to do the best we can on this day. (Some days will be better than others!) We support ourselves with thoughts of self-confidence and self-affirmation, and utilize the support of our friends.

But there are other coping skills we can develop in facing our anxieties: confronting ourselves; taking a break; getting our composure back; being compassionate; understanding and forgiving ourselves; exercise, especially walking. We need to find ways to relax our uptight bodies. We need to keep our expectations about others, ourselves, and situations realistic; know our limitations, be strict with limiting the time we think about a problem, and keep issues in perspective and balance; be grateful for the good things in our lives and lessen the emotional energy we are putting forth; and, finally, to consult a doctor if anxiety is overwhelming us physically and emotionally.

RELIGIOUS ANXIETIES

Let me say a bit about the anxieties that emerge from thinking wrongly about religion. These anxieties are most damaging to a wholesome faith in God because they disrupt our peace of soul, which religion is supposed to foster. Such anxieties distance our relationship with God and stunt our spiritual development. They will aggravate our other emotional anxieties, like depression.

Religious anxieties emerge from first, a negative and fearful image of God; second, from obsession with sin; and third, from the vast amount of misunderstanding and misinterpretations of both the Christian message and the teachings of the Church. All of the above breed religious anxiety. One answer to alleviating these anxieties is massive, pervasive, and relevant religious education for adults, that moves people out of an eighth-grade knowledge of their faith and assists them to think more clearly about their religion. This has the potential to free adults from religious anxieties, enabling them to reach religious maturity and develop an informed conscience.

Christians can also eliminate their religious anxieties by believing in a loving, merciful, and forgiving God as taught by Jesus. They need to stop seeing mortal sin here, there, and everywhere. Indeed, sin does exist, but we need to develop a more real and balanced sense of sin. The sin Jesus talks about in the gospels is about relationships, hurting others, failing to do good, or neglecting others in our lives every day. The proper understanding of serious sin will mean that we won't get caught up or tormented by the idea that mortal sin can be committed by missing Mass or by cursing or by a long list of such "sins" that have nothing to do with the real sin. True guilt flows from hurting and neglecting others, and other acts we perpetuate on each other.

Since Vatican II the increase of knowledge about theology and information about Scripture has been remarkable. Teachers need to disseminate this wonderful and freeing information. The choice is ours. Do we want to learn more and be free or are we content with the status quo? Do we prefer the darkness that breeds anxieties, or do we want the light that shows us the Way? "Do we want to be healed?" is the perennial question of Jesus.

Not all of our anxieties will go away. We are born into anxieties; they are part of life. How we handle them makes the difference. We cannot let them continually overwhelm us and control us or we will never be free persons. Our lives must be filled with prayers of trust, which can bring us hope and make us optimistic people. The Bible tells us, "Fear not" 365 times, once for each day in the year. As Jesus said, "Fear is useless; what is needed is trust" (Luke 8:50).

11.

Remarriage

In discussing the reality of divorce it is important to consider the issue of remarriage. Some people marry soon after being divorced, others marry many years later, while some choose to remain single. Many first marriages fail, while almost two-thirds of second marriages fail. This latter statistic is surprising. Many believe that if a person has failed in one marriage he or she will learn from mistakes made and have a greater chance of succeeding in a second marriage. But it seems to require about three to five years before a person recovers emotionally and psychologically from a divorce. If they have not acquired any insight or any understanding as to why their first marriage failed then the length of years between divorce and remarriage won't matter.

People jeopardize their chances of successful second marriage because they lack the necessary information about how or why they failed in their first marriage. Even though people think they are prepared to remarry, they often don't realize they are still wounded by their past failure, and so they carry unresolved baggage into a second marriage. That is why, for such people, counseling is necessary in order to shed light on the failed marriage.

WHY DID MY FIRST MARRIAGE FAIL?

The following questions may assist a divorced person reflect on a former marriage and acquire information about their emotional and psychological readiness to remarry.

- How did I fail in the marriage?
- Am I healing from my failed marriage?
- Am I able to choose to remarry or to remain single, and, in either case, realize that I am a whole, healthy person? Being a whole person means feeling complete and fulfilled as a person, not needing someone else to make me feel complete.

When these questions are faced and answered honestly, there is the possibility of a successful second marriage.

1. *Why did my first marriage fail?* This question looks at the dynamics of the marriage. Did we communicate honestly? Were there destructive patterns of relating? For example, if the marriage was continually conflictual, what were the issues? How did we argue, appropriately or inappropriately? Or did we avoid conflict? Did we resort to blaming and/or name-calling? Did we resolve issues or reach a compromise? Was silence a factor? What type of conflict resolution did we apply? If not, why not? How did we express or not express anger? Was there a power struggle going on? How did our parents deal with conflict? Did one partner come from a family where conflict was allowed and another from a family that avoided conflict at any cost? Were there any addictions?

Such questions and reflections are bound to identify unhealthy patterns of relating, as well as surface the underlying causes that eventually destroyed the relationship or prevented it from ever developing into a permanent relationship. The information acquired will usually go beyond the marriage and will necessarily focus on families of origin where some will rec- ognize they are adult children of alcoholics and very dysfunctional families.

It takes courage for one to face up to one's own mistakes.

2. *How did I fail in the marriage?* It's easy for one of the spouses to identify the faults, wrong behavior, or ineptitude of the other spouse. However, it takes courage and honesty for one to face up to one's own mistakes and inadequacies. Taking responsibility for how *I* failed in the marriage is the ultimate goal. Knowing how the other person failed is necessary, but the more important question is: how did I fail?

How did I deal with my spouse and with difficulties and problems? Did I respond appropriately, remain silent, or overreact? Did I allow the other spouse to undermine my self-confidence and self-esteem? Did I allow that spouse to control me?

This questioning can be painful as well as informative. How will one chart a better direction in the future without this absolutely essential information? The broken marriage, as disappointing as it may be, is indeed a treasure chest of vital information and understanding about my past and myself.

Many people were never genuine and independent individuals in their marriage. Many, because of counseling and hard work, have made the journey through divorce, and emerged for the first time in their lives as persons who know who they are. I have seen divorced clients, especially divorced women, who possessed little or no self-esteem, self-love, or self-confidence before they married, and who lost what little sense of self they had during the marriage. It took a divorce to make them free and whole. They had entered the marriage with such a poor self-image that they were programmed to make a poor choice of a husband. But now, after the divorce, they are able to make a better choice of a partner.

A marriage with communication problems can assume various patterns. One such pattern is the quiet, smiling, and always-agreeable wife married to a husband who talks too much, listens little, and controls the wife. He perceives his smiling, quiet wife as happy and content. For example, Joanne became involved with George, her

How am I healing? What have I learned about myself?

husband Peter's business partner. When Joanne suddenly leaves Peter and moves in with George, Peter is shocked, devastated. He feels hurt, angry, and betrayed, and cries out, "How could she do this to me?" Never having heard any criticism or complaint against him from Joanne, Peter saw himself as a loving and caring husband and father. He proclaims proudly, "I took care of her and the family, provided for them financially, never ran around or drank." He saw only his goodness and caring in the face of her betrayal.

The seemingly one-sided failure of this marriage is the responsibility of both partners. Joanne's real problems were her lack of self-confidence, low self-esteem, and her fear of communicating honestly, and expressing her anger, especially toward men. Thus, she avoided conflicts by being submissive. Over the years of her marriage to Peter she had built up a tremendous amount of resentment toward his controlling manner, and, eventually, she lost any respect, love, and trust for him—as she gradually lost respect for herself. Her involvement with George is a result of her unresolved conflicts with and anger toward her husband Peter, which had never been addressed with him.

Peter, on the other hand, is parading around as the victim, and is totally blind to his own controlling and insensitive behavior in his marriage. He deludes himself into thinking he was the perfect mate. Peter failed to be aware that Joanne's silence was not an indicator that she was happy with him. In fact, he never really knew what she thought, or felt, or needed. He assumed that she was happy. Peter was not in touch with what Joanne felt or with her emotional needs, nor was he aware of her lack of self-confidence and low self-esteem. Indeed, he actually thrived on those qualities of Joanne's because he was so insecure himself.

The above example is one of a typical failed marriage, where the symptoms of unfaithfulness are not the real issue. A marriage can be successful only when both partners acknowledge and understand their own weaknesses, change their behavior, and grow in order to develop a healthy, functional relationship. Even if there is no reconciliation between the two spouses they still need to resolve their issues and gain insight into them before they can possibly attempt a second marriage and expect it to succeed. If they persist in their blindness and gain no insight into themselves they will condemn themselves to a second failure in marriage, or at best, to a second-rate marriage.

3. *How am I healing?* What have I learned about myself? Two or three years after the divorce the persons involved need to be able to understand the causes of the failed marriage. They should possess information and insights into their participation in the relationship that failed. Also of importance is the necessity for both parties to understand their family of origin, and to gather from them the vital information that is connected to their failed marriage. What were the good and bad patterns of relating that I learned in my family? How did I relate to my parents and siblings? How did my parents relate to each other, the fundamental blueprint of my understanding of marriage? What were the emotional weaknesses and strengths of both parents that I brought into the marriage, and did I bring into it unresolved conflicts with my parents? What was the quality of communication, not only between my parents but also between my parents and me? Were we a closed, enmeshed family or a conflictual, disengaged family?

People will relive their past in three ways:

1. They repeat the failures of their family. "Dad was an alcoholic. I married an alcoholic."

2. They rebel against their past. "My parents constantly fought and overreacted angrily with each other, so I vowed never to fight or to express my anger."

3. They can rebuild on the good they learned from their family and work to avoid any weaknesses they may have been exposed to.

Changing involves bringing new information into life and relationships. Thus we can break the unhealthy cycle of the past.

Divorced people know they are healing when their intense feelings of hurt, anger, rage, and revenge are less intense and more diffused, when fears and anxieties about themselves and their children recede and are replaced by confidence and hope. There is a sense of their being in a better place and being more responsible for their lives. Blaming is not an issue anymore; the past is no longer controlling their emotions. There is even a sense of gratitude that they have made it through the dark valley of divorce. Some will even rejoice and be grateful that a destructive marriage is over, and they can say that the marriage should never have taken place. For some, there is a renaissance. As a woman said to me, "If it had not been for the divorce I would never have become the person God destined me to be."

What divorced people need to realize is that, after obtaining a legal divorce, the emotional, psychological divorce will require more time and effort. Many people have never attained psychological divorce. They hold on to hate and anger. In a sense, they are still married because hate and anger imply the continued existence of a relationship to the former spouse. Conflicts can continue over finances, children, and other unresolved issues. Because of all this, mediation and especially counseling are imperative for divorcing people.

Sometimes, divorced people remarry with these feelings and issues still unresolved so that they are living in two marriages. The second marriage will have a difficult time surviving because one or both spouses are still enmeshed in the first marriage with all its destructive elements. These will undermine the second marriage and prevent it from flourishing as a healthy relationship.

Young children and, even more so, older ones, can become a source of stress and divisiveness in a new marriage. Problems from the former marriage can drain off emotional energy sorely needed in the second marriage. People may never come to a solid and workable game plan with regard to children, finances, and other heldover issues connected with the former spouse or family. These issues need to be discussed and worked through before people remarry or else they may cause disaster in a second marriage.

Another sign that divorced persons are healing and ready to remarry is that they are able to forgive the other partner, accept God's forgiveness, and forgive themselves. When we forgive a former spouse we do that primarily for our own sake and for our own healing. It doesn't mean we won't experience painful feelings about a former spouse at times. It doesn't mean we have to take the former spouse back or be reconciled with him or her. Forgiveness doesn't mean that we condone the wrongs done by the other. Rather, forgiving means we are able to let go and move on with our lives.

We forgive for our own sake and healing.

The promise of the future is before us. All that has happened to us has transformed us. We have become persons of hope who are better, not bitter. Our self-knowledge has been enhanced by the insights we have gained from the divorce experience and from counseling. We have changed and have a better relationship with ourselves. We have more confidence and trust in ourselves, which allows us to have better trust and confidence in others, which leads to making better choices in our relationships.

4. *Am I able to choose to remarry or remain single, and, in either case, realize that I am a whole, healthy person?* The goal of divorce is not remarriage, but healing and finding peace, contentment, and happiness within myself. Happiness is a personal choice not found in another person, but in myself.

If divorced people remarry it will be a free choice, not based on a desperate need to *have* someone so that I can *be* someone. Remarriage should not be motivated by loneliness or fear of being alone, or out of a need for someone to take care of me or my need to take care of someone else. It must be a choice that is made because the other person and I want to form a close, loving relationship with the right person—a relationship in which we can share our lives together.

An important aspect of the remarriage issue demands that the person I am marrying has healed, if divorced or widowed, has done the necessary grieving work, and can adequately answer these four questions:

1. Does the person have insight into the former marriage and his or her family of origin?

2. Does the person take responsibility for his or her part in the failure of the first marriage?

3. Has the person changed? Is he or she working on change, gaining insight, self-knowledge, and motivation?

4. Are bitterness, anger, and blame controlling his or her life?

If the person I want to marry does not give adequate answers to these questions, then no matter how good a candidate he or she may otherwise seem to be, or how strong my attraction to such a person is, then my advice is, don't do it! There is no hope of a successful relationship; it is doomed to fail before the vows are pronounced. If a person is willing to seek premarital counseling, that is a positive sign. However, I need to stand back and wait for the counseling to take effect before saying "I do."

In my experience, many divorced clients, after they had healed and gone on with their lives, have brought their prospective husbands or wives to me for counseling. They would not remarry until the prospective spouse was willing to take an honest look at him or herself, their former marriage, and their families. If a possible new mate is truly serious, they will follow through with seeking any necessary help. Words and promises are not enough. What is necessary is action and change. A second marriage is difficult enough for two people who have sufficient understanding about themselves to remarry and who promise to work at their relationship. It is extremely precarious when one or both spouses show no understanding of their former marital relationships and are driven by some emotional high, neediness, or other neurotic reasons.

Sometimes a failed second marriage is followed by third or fourth marriages, which also fail. Sometimes the failure occurs because the spouses are not willing to seek genuine emotional intimacy, which is very demanding. They are willing to settle for less in the area of intimacy—and less is not enough for a successful marriage.

Frequently I've had discussions with divorced women who are dating and feel forced into a sexual relationship before they are prepared. I've seen such relationships fail because the sexual relationship was not rooted in a sound emotional and psychological relationship. Women complain bitterly and with great frustration that there's no possibility of "finding a man" unless they are willing to sleep with him on the first date. All this indicates is that neither person is ready for any serious relationship. The man who is desperate to have his own needs met probably feels inadequate, and may be feeling the need to control the other. He is not listening to the woman who is talking about waiting before they become sexually involved.

Sometimes women give in to such sexual demands because of their own neediness and inadequate feelings, or from the fear that they might not be able to find another mate. Self-respect is compromised, submissiveness and control become an issue, and anxiety and unrealistic expectations follow. These and many other variations of the same theme are all characteristics of people who are definitely not ready for any type of serious, emotional, psychological intimacy.

Many women have been effective motivators in persuading men to take a serious look at their failed relationships. Some men, for the first time in their lives, really come to grips with their feelings and the gamut of emotional difficulties that so many men have. Dr. James A. Schaller's book, *Become the Husband Your Wife Thought She Married*, examines this subject well.

One of the statements we hear from prospective candidates for remarriage is how they are in agreement on so many questions. That's good, but of even greater importance is how they surface and deal with the areas of their differences. How do they remain individuals with differences and remain together? Can they engage in open and honest communication, disagree, express their anger, and have appropriate conflict?

Remaining Single

"Can I remain single and still see myself as a whole person?" is a vital question. If such a choice is made one must realize there is no stigma or disgrace to remaining single. It is a lifestyle and a vocation in itself. The freedom it affords provides opportunities in life for such things as further education, careers, and social and religious service to others. The possibilities and opportunities for meaningful involvements are many.

Remaining single doesn't mean not having emotionally close and intimate relationships with others, whether men or women. We all need emotional intimacy, no matter what state of life we choose. Nor is it a fear of remarriage, or fear of failure again, or of feeling inadequate, that prevents a person from remarrying. It is simply a choice made to accept a single life because of the meaning and the opportunities it provides. It is a matter of feeling good about oneself and having a good relationship with oneself.

Sometimes family and friends bring pressure to remarry on those who have chosen to remain single. The single persons themselves are quite comfortable with their state of life—but family and friends are not! The single person needs to remain convinced and confident about the single state, so that, eventually, family and friends back off.

Single people need to be comfortable in the presence of married couples and not see themselves as outcasts or out of place. A single person may have to deal with couples who see the single person as a threat to their marriage. The single person may also have to address the suspicion of others who think they may be strange or gay.

Over the years, I have seen many divorced people, especially women, who, after recovery from divorce, are healed and are genuinely happy with being single. They have no interest in remarriage. What is very evident is their self-confidence, their sense of self, their satisfaction with life and themselves. They have goals in their lives, goals they are actively seeking to realize. They are an inspiration and moral support to their children.

Whatever direction divorced persons take, it must be freely chosen, and this free choice can only happen when they have processed their failed marriage, thrown overboard past baggage, and found emotional and spiritual healing. They also need to feel good about themselves, forgive themselves and others, and have a sense of being whole persons.

What Is a Catholic Annulment?

The issue of a Church annulment is a particular problem for many Catholics, and an enigma for Protestants! An annulment states that a particular marriage was never, from the wedding day on, a sacramental marriage. A civil marriage—yes (thus any children will be legitimate); a sacramental marriage, no. A sacramental marriage is a union of hearts and minds and bodies entered into for life. Some people are incapable of entering into such a union—for example, they may be emotionally or psychologically immature or damaged, or they may be alcoholics or drug addicts at the time of the marriage.

The annulment process uncovers the reasons why a particular

marriage is not a sacramental one, and, based on these findings, the Church annuls the marriage—i.e., declares it never was a sacramental marriage. The annulment does not say the spouses are bad people. But it does say that the annulled marriage never had the capacity to become a Christian marriage—that is, a permanent and life-giving relationship.

There are other technical reasons why a marriage may be annulled. For example, some Church law concerning marriage was not followed thus making it invalid. Another reason for an annulment occurs if moral pressure was put on a person to marry, thus limiting that person's freedom to act.

It is not uncommon for Catholics who have received an annulment to remarry, and to have serious problems in their second marriage. A Church annulment is not some miraculous antidote that prevents a second marriage from failing. Many Catholic dioceses are now requiring that, after an annulment is granted, counseling be required before a second marriage can take place. In Philadelphia, for example, the archdiocese has developed a program that provides assistance and support to those considering remarriage after an annulment—a highly commendable action on the Church's part and one that should be followed by all dioceses.

Only a small percentage, about ten percent, of divorced Catholics in the U.S. apply for an annulment, and usually, eight-five percent of those who seek an annulment are granted one. Why then do so few Catholics apply for an annulment?

First, there is widespread ignorance and misunderstanding about what a Church annulment is, and false information about the length of time it takes to obtain an annulment (it usually takes from one to two years). Others don't want to go through the whole painful story of a failed marriage again, and find the questions they are required to answer too invasive or personal. There is also the belief among Catholics that an annulment costs a lot of money. This misinformation can be fueled by real or rumored stories that prominent or wealthy Catholics obtained annulments quickly because of their social or moneyed status. Usually the required fee requested by a marriage tribunal barely covers the cost of the secretarial work involved. Serious consideration is given to financial hardship cases

> *The Christian community needs to be a place of healing.*

and the fee may be reduced or even dropped entirely. The cost of a legal divorce is astronomical when compared to the meager fee asked for an annulment.

I have cautioned Catholics not to be anxious about seeking an annulment until after they have journeyed through a certain amount of counseling. If they do this they will be much better prepared to seek an annulment. Furthermore, they need to focus on their woundedness and find some healing after the first marriage's failure. This process is much more important than an annulment. I reassure them that the majority of people who seek an annulment will get it. To be precise, if a marriage tribunal accepts a case, the annulment will almost certainly go through.

Some Catholics resent the voluminous amount of writing that seems necessary to answer some of the questions on the annulment forms. Often people do write extensively, but miss the point or the crux of the marriage failure and of one's part in that failure. A professional counselor could provide the necessary guidance to a person, guidance that will help the person to expedite and isolate the pertinent reasons why the marriage failed. At the same time in counseling, the petitioner is gathering information which will indicate possible psychological problems that existed before the marriage and which helped cause the demise of the marriage.

Tribunal officials must be responsible in choosing those who will assist them in the work of processing annulments. It has been my experience that most priests and deacons and tribunal officials are people of sensitivity, aware of the hurt the people with whom they are dealing are suffering. They take seriously their responsibility to reflect the compassion, mercy, and understanding of Christ. As you can see, there is a great need to educate Catholics in matters concerning annulments. The fact that so few Catholics apply for an annulment may indicate just how much ignorance and misinformation about the annulment process exists.

All that having been said, the truth is that the Catholic Church must face the fact that the annulment process is not working effectively. I believe that what is needed is a re-examination and an overhauling of the whole process. After my years of working with divorced people I am convinced that the following procedure may want to be considered by Church officials as a possible outline for the renovation of the annulment process.

1. Professional counseling must be required for all those seeking an annulment. Dioceses could provide that service for a reasonable fee.

2. The counselor, with permission of the client and even accompanied by the client, must make a report to the diocesan marriage tribunal. This report would lead to a discussion and the answers to the four questions I posed earlier in this chapter. The tribunal could eventually make a response about the possibility of remarriage based upon the person's insights.

3. The diocese must continue to provide support groups for the divorced and separated. These groups help people experience emotional and spiritual healing and affirmation. The diocese could also offer workshops on the psychology of marriage relationships, on the family, and on the emotional-psychological aspects of the human person.

4. Finally, the diocesan marriage tribunal must focus more on the psychological-spiritual healing of the divorced rather than on legal aspects.

These steps may need to be clarified and developed, but they are, I think, the basis of a much more wholesome, less threatening, and more efficient and Christ-like pastoral approach to annulment than the heavily laden juridical process prevalent today. Furthermore, my approach would be less threatening to non-Catholics who need an annulment because it provides a healing and helping approach to a second Christian marriage. The Church then becomes a haven of support and understanding for divorced and separated people, as well as an advocate for promoting healthier and happier second marriages. Again, the whole annulment process should be addressed more pastorally than legalistically.

The reception of the Eucharist is a problem for those Catholics who cannot get an annulment for whatever reason, and who remarry in a non-Catholic ceremony or civilly. Other Catholics never attempt to seek an annulment. The issue for most of these Catholics becomes a matter of personal conscience with regard to the reception of the Eucharist. These people are not legally out of the Church but are told by the Church they cannot receive the Eucharist because they are not validly married in a Catholic ceremony. Still, many of them receive the Eucharist because they feel that they have a right to the Eucharist and have made a decision of conscience on their own. Rightly or wrongly we must admit that this is common current thinking and behavior among many Catholics today.

The agony of divorce and remarriage is painful enough without adding "religious pain" to it. The Christian community needs to be a place of solace, comfort, and healing for people experiencing divorce and remarriage. The inn to which the Good Samaritan brought the man who had been attacked is a metaphor for the Church, where those who have been robbed of their dreams of a happy marriage may seek solace and wisdom. When they leave the haven of the inn they will be strong enough to continue their journey through life.

The two basic human urges are first, to be connected with another person so as to be able to relate closely to that person and to be and second, the urge to be a unique person in charge of one's life; able to direct that life. Marriage is probably one of the best ways to satisfy both these urges. It is a sophisticated process in which people can grow and develop as individuals, and, at the same time, find the connection they desire. The tension between maintaining the self and maintaining the relationship is a healthy tension that makes for the creative power of marriage. This can bring men and women reasonable satisfaction in this life and salvation in the next.

Note: For more information, I recommend *Remarriage in the Church After Divorce: Pastoral Solutions*, published by the Association for the Rights of Catholics in the Church (ARCC), P.O. Box 85, Southampton, MA 01073.

12.

Making Marriage Work

Marriage answers the deep urge that most people possess to be intimately connected with another and to bear children. It guarantees the continuation of the human race, and provides the greatest opportunity for a woman and man to find emotional and sexual intimacy.

Marriage has had its variations, good and bad, throughout human history. It has evolved and developed, but it still has a way to go in the matter of spousal abuse and of inequality between men and women. As people strive in marriage to be together yet different, there is an ongoing natural tension, which is the dynamic of the intimate relationship they seek. Marriage has been problematic from the beginning, when Adam and Eve broke their trusting relationship with God and with each

What do I need to change in myself?

other. Adam blamed Eve and Eve blamed the serpent. All this sounds familiar to people who are trying to get marriage right.

Some people attempt marriage two or more times in an attempt to make it work, so great is the urge to be married and find intimacy. In spite of the sophisticated education men and women enjoy today they still often lack the information, understanding, and insights that are available in regard to developing good relationships. Young people are still marrying as their parents did, often continuing to live out the good and bad aspects of their parents' marriage.

Today there is a lot of pessimism about marriage, much apprehension about being able to remain married and maintain a long-term relationship. This pessimism appears in the sort of writing in which the writer calls marriage a trap for men and women. It is reflected in the delayed approach by some to marriage in order that they might be free to enjoy the single life. Then there's the hesitation to commit, which results in couples living together without benefit of matrimony and the fear of developing intimacy, which leads many to settle for unfulfilling sexual encounters. Young people, seeing so many unhappy married people and the number of failed marriages, understandably question their chances of succeeding in marriage. Often they can develop a cynical outlook on marriage, which leads them to delay marrying.

I would hope that, after reading the previous chapters, we could be more positive about the possibility that there can be good and lasting marriages. As such, here are five characteristics of a good marriage. I think these five characteristics sum up most of what I've been saying because they include the essential features of a good, functioning marital relationship.

First, there is the need for each spouse to take responsibility for making the marriage work. This requires that each partner focuses on their own part in the marriage and be accountable for carrying out what they need to do. Each should consider these questions: What are my roles in the marriage? What must I do to maintain and improve this marriage? How do I come to know my partner and enhance my partner's life? This approach places the responsibility for making the marriage work on the shoulders of each spouse. It means making time for the other person, and initiating the move to take time to be together. Christian marriage is about serving the other and the giving of oneself. It's about laying down one's life for another.

To focus on one's responsibility in the marriage means taking responsibility for one's failures, e.g., one's neglect of the other, one's part in the problems that occur, or seeing one's role in any disharmony that occurs in the relationship. As a spouse, I need to be able to focus on how I respond to the other's hurt, anger, meanness, neglect, or abuse. I can choose to respond in a balanced and appropriate manner or I can overreact, blame, or become defensive. When I allow the other partner to get to me, lessen my self-confidence, or lower my self-esteem, I need to ask, how did this happen? What do I need to change in myself? Tony Hendra speaks beautifully about listening in his touching, autobiographical book, *Father Joe: the Man Who Saved My Soul.* "The only way to know each other, is to listen. Listening is reaching out into that unknown other self, surmounting your walls and theirs; listening is the beginning of understanding, the first exercise of love."

In the end how I behave in a marriage is my choice. My happiness in the marital relationship is my responsibility, not the responsibility of the other partner—a common error made in marriage. A happy marriage is the combination and connection of two happy persons.

The second characteristic of a successful marriage is the development of the art and skills of clear communication, which include effective listening. Again, it is each spouse's responsibility to develop communication skills, even though the other spouse may be a poor communicator or an inattentive listener. Each must be committed to communicating consistently, no matter how bad things may be. It often happens that when one spouse is lacking in communication skills this can eventually affect the other spouse in a negative way, e.g., to become less of a communicator. This is when the spouse who communicates well needs to be persistent and confident, which will eventually bear fruit, or else the relationship will truly suffer.

There are three rules for communication. First, communicate. Second, communicate. Third, after all is said and done, communicate. Communication in a marriage goes beyond verbal communication. It is inherent in the multiple aspects of body language as well as in the sexual communication between spouses. Are we aware of our spouse's thoughts, feelings, and moods, in touch with and willingly listening to them? Conflict will naturally result from some communication, but this is all part of genuine communication. Silence is the real killer of marriages.

Being a focused and intense listener means being in touch with and responsive to what the other person is saying, thinking, feeling, and needing. It means being aware of the whole being of the other person. This is when empathy for the other is developed, and connectedness and healing takes place in a relationship. With this open and honest communication and intent listening a lasting trust develops, which leads to emotional, psychological, and sexual intimacy. There is a sense that one is being cared for, respected, and thought of as important to the other.

The third characteristic of a successful marriage is the need for spouses to have a deep sense of hope that the marriage will survive no matter what happens. Hope is the conviction that things can be different in a marriage, that things can be better. Hope develops the ability to cope, and the more spouses cope the more hope they will have. The hopeful attitude of one spouse will affect the other spouse when they may be getting discouraged by problems or difficulties.

The fourth necessary characteristic is the presence and the promise of forgiveness. You could almost say that this quality makes a Christian marriage what it is. People in a marriage will fail one another occasionally. Couples will experience disappointment and hurt. Married people need to be realistic about the fact that these failures will happen time and time again. Expressed forgiveness must be an essential aspect of any marriage if that marriage is to heal and grow.

Forgiveness not only heals a wounded relationship, it also brings spouses closer together. From this experience they learn more about themselves, about each other's goodness and brokenness.

Finally, all these characteristics of a good marriage are fortified and unified by the commitment of the spouses to make the marriage work, to keep on trying in spite of failures, discouragement, and frustrations. It is this consistency and determination that not only energize the marriage, but develop an atmosphere of trust between the spouses. Often one spouse may make an obvious effort to improve the marriage. This can have a positive influence on the other spouse and make him or her work harder at the marriage, which in turn, will build a stronger trust between the spouses.

Trust is the foundation of marriage.

Trust is the foundation of marriage. No matter what happens, a married person should be able to rely on the other to be present in good times as well as in bad. What a sense of security this can bring to a marriage! This type of commitment involves the personal resolve that each spouse has to take responsibility for making the marriage work. In these times of rampant individualism such an attitude is rare because people are so immersed in their own needs and rights. If this is the case a marriage becomes more "me" than "we." A good marriage includes the possibility of having both "me" and "we" fulfilled. But this requires continual work, effort, cooperation, adjustments, communication, and, yes, even conflict. With these five characteristics, a good marriage is possible, and love becomes a reality.

Marriage is a committed relationship. Love in marriage is a decision to love, whether one always feels love or not. Sexual love not only strengthens the bond of love but gives comfort and pleasure in the midst of the stresses of married life.

It has been shown in research that marriages founded on religious beliefs and practice have a greater chance of surviving and thriving. A spouse's committed religious belief and practice strengthens a marital commitment, and motivates the spouses to stay the course and to work out their difficulties. Their awareness of God's presence in their lives and in their problems gives meaning and hope to their marriage. This is God's grace at work in the marriage.

There are no perfect marriages because there are no perfect people. But the five qualities of a good marriage I have mentioned can provide the tools that can assist married people through their own marital journey. They can strengthen the spouses' promise to hang in and remain faithful to one another, "in sickness and in health, in good times and bad, for richer, for poorer, until death do us part."

As I conclude this chapter on the five qualities of a good marriage, I would like to recommend a book entitled *Good Marriage, Bad Marriage*, by Les and Leslie Parrott, who are Christian marriage counselors. They discuss in this book some of the ideas I have mentioned and expanded on.

13.

Family

The foundational social unit is the family, which has its origin in the early stages of the human race. It is the common factor uniting all cultures. Families are the building blocks of any society and guarantee the propagation of the human race. The strength and durability of any society stems from the cohesiveness of its families.

The question is, how do we preserve and strengthen family life? Every culture and society has its own built-in laws, traditions, and taboos aimed at preserving family life. In the Western world we possess valuable social and psychological studies that are all, for the most part, in agreement with Judeo-Christian values of the family. In this chapter I want to highlight certain basic dynamics necessary for the preservation and enhancement of family life.

COMMUNICATION

The first dynamic necessary for a family to acquire unity and be functional is effective communication among all members of the family. Parents are encouraged to continually talk with their children, even from their earliest days. Such talk with a baby is like breathing life into the child. It comes alive and responds. The talk of the parents helps the infant to come to realize its own separateness and identity. Parents' communication with each other is not only essential for their relationship, it serves as an example for their children. Parents set the tone for family communication, the lifeblood that flows through the body to preserve it and give it life. Communication brings about family connectedness and awareness.

Communication must encompass all situations and realities in a family. It must be direct and clear, open and honest. Communication helps family members share what they perceive, what they think, what they feel, and to express needs they might have. It is only in such an open environment that people can come to know each other and begin to connect with each other. This doesn't mean that they necessarily agree with each other, but that they have shared with one another as a unit, as a connected group.

Indirect communication occurs, for example, when a son tells his mother what he should be telling his father. The mother in turn speaks to the father, which disturbs him because his son did not trust him enough to speak directly to him. Such indirect communication undermines family unity and trust. We call such indirect communication "triangulation." After listening to her son, the mother needs to encourage him to speak directly to his father or else she enables dysfunctional communication.

Often in family counseling sessions, when a family is discussing a family situation, members reveal that there are different perceptions of that situation. Much of a family's presenting problem is usually locked up in these different views, which up until now the family has not shared. They do not understand each other or the issue under discussion, and so they may develop unnecessary feelings of anger or misunderstanding, which have caused them to be distant and disconnected from each other.

As mentioned earlier, the main goal of communication is not resolution but revelation. Communication gives people the opportunity to reveal themselves, and very often it is in the revelation of what they perceive, think, feel, and need that they find resolution of a problem. Resolution doesn't necessarily mean a solution to a problem, however, although it can be. It doesn't necessarily mean agreement, but it means at least that the groundwork is now prepared for people to negotiate, cooperate, compromise, and tolerate each other.

Everyone has to be heard and given the chance to speak.

All members of the family must participate in communicating. Some will speak more than others, but no one member should be allowed to dominate, and no member should be allowed to hide behind silence. The family atmosphere must proclaim that all have permission to speak and to say what they think, feel, or need.

Parents need to take a leadership role so they know what everyone thinks and feels about issues. Everyone has to be heard and given the chance to speak, even the youngest children. Only then can the parents make realistic decisions or suggestions about matters pertaining to the family.

It is in this type of family communication that family members learn the skills of talking with one another and the art of listening. In such an atmosphere, people learn emotional connectedness and experience family intimacy when they share, on the deepest levels, their pain, joy, sorrows, affection, anger, fears, regrets, failures, and successes. Family members learn to live with disagreement, different opinions, and personality differences. This experience of communicating helps family members develop the skills to form their own relationships in their own lives. The communication skills learned in the family are then carried out into life. Many people are not able to form or maintain relationships. They lack the necessary skills because they did not learn them in their families.

Everyone needs to identify the skills of communication and listening they learned or did not learn in their families, and to sort out the bad and good aspects of communicating in their own family.

They need to discard bad communicating habits and develop good habits while they learn more about effective communication and listening from the abundant material available today. Too often, it is only when family or marital discord arises that people begin to address their problems in communication, then seek the counseling and information they need. Everyone has the God-given capacity to communicate and to listen, and to improve listening skills.

CONFLICT

The other dynamic that is a reality in any family is conflict. Conflict will especially be present when family members communicate in an open and honest way, with direct and clear communication that not only clarifies issues, but surfaces disagreements, as well. As painful and as difficult as this conflict may be, it makes for a healthier and better functioning family.

How often we have heard of so-called "quiet" families suddenly exploding into deadly violence? Given the lack of communicating, it was bound to happen. Or perhaps the family may manifest other problems, physical or psychological, that are symptomatic of underlying conflicts.

A certain amount of conflict will be necessary to preserve a family and keep its members connected. (We are again talking about appropriate conflict, and not about violence or physical or emotional abuse, which make up conflict that is out of control.) Children need to learn early in their families that both fair conflict and appropriate anger are an essential part of a healthy, functioning family, and that they are a normal part of living. Only with the guidance of parents who understand and engage in appropriate conflict themselves can children learn to integrate conflict and anger into their lives and relationships.

In families where anger and conflict are permitted and monitored, people can eventually establish their own identity. Members of families where the members are so enmeshed with each other that they are excessively agreeable and pleasing, but who don't have their own opinions, are afraid to express them, or avoid any disharmony at any cost, cannot mature and grow emotionally. They are clones of one another. On the other hand, families that are in continual and destructive conflict are wounded, and they will live out unresolved conflict and anger with other people in their lives.

SELF-CONFIDENCE

The dynamic characteristics of self-confidence are the foundation of a sense of security in the family. Parents today are under a lot of pressure from society, a society with values that may be contrary to the parents. Parents without self-confidence, and who also don't agree with each other, may give their children a confusing message or no message at all on questions of value. In a sense, this is a kind of abandonment and emotional neglect. If parents are unsure of themselves they can easily cave in to their children's questionable demands or just take a back seat in their children's lives, leaving their children rudderless and confused, because they are unsure what to do or what to say.

All parents will make their share of mistakes, but the confidence good parents have in themselves will contribute to the security children will appreciate, even if they don't verbalize it. They may even express anger at their parents or disagree with them. Confident parents produce confident children. Anxious parents produce anxious children who are unsure of themselves. Children need firm, guiding direction from their parents in order to grow into healthy, self-confident adults.

CONTROL AND CONSISTENCY

There is a powerful dynamic of parental control and consistency that flows from the aforementioned dynamics. Healthy parental control involves the parents having an overall awareness of their children; of who they are and where they are, of what's going on in their lives, and of what they think, feel, and need. It means that the parents are present to their children, talking to them and, above all, listening to them. It means being able to say no and deal with their arguments, anger, and whining.

Control is supported by consistency, meaning that the parents act, think, and behave in a predictable manner. They are not controlled by mood swings or erratic changes of thinking and reasoning, all of which are very confusing to children. In the home there is order, scheduling, and boundaries so that children know what to expect from their parents. This develops a sense of security in the children and a trust in their parents. Flexibility is possible in such a family, but only when it is inherent in an otherwise consistent home atmosphere.

Children will be inconsistent and will have mood swings, especially in the teen-years. The parents need to be in control of themselves so as not to be sucked in by their children's erratic behavior. Children need structure, boundaries, and limits from their parents. The children will test parents in many ways, which is normal, but parents need to realize this, deal with it, and insist on the disciplinary question at issue. Consequences need to follow on misbehavior, and all of the above needs to be accompanied by dialogue with the children that clarifies what has happened. Where such an atmosphere of openness is not present, there will be insecurity manifested by chaotic behavior, anxieties, and anger.

Discipline is a caring, loving experience that children need. Discipline doesn't necessarily mean punishing, as many adults think. The word comes from the Latin word *discere*, which means to teach, train, lead. Discipline has become a lost art among many parents, who are often reacting against the severe and rigid discipline of their own childhood. They now opt not to discipline at all and so they enable their children by over-indulgence and over-permissiveness. All this, in turn, produces children who are anxious, unsure of themselves, and unhappy as well as angry and often out of control.

Control and consistency by parents establishes an atmosphere of order; and where there is order, love, trust, and relationships can grow. Rules and regulations without a relationship lead to rebellion. Disciplined parents—parents who have control over their own lives—can discipline their children. Be in control of yourself first, and then you can be in control of your children.

COMMITMENT

Finally, the dynamic that gives energy, meaning, and motivation to all of the above is a sense of commitment. Commitment involves dedication to the family and determination to make it work, with each member doing their own part. Each member of the family, from the youngest to the oldest, has the responsibility to make the family functional. That's commitment. The family is a system, and all the persons in the family are essential to the working of the system. "One for all and all for one" should be every family's motto. Everyone's behavior—good or bad—has an effect on the family system. It is within such a family that members gain a sense of belonging and of feeling worthwhile, while gaining a sense of their own identity. We all have two urges: to have a relationship with a significant other and to be one's own unique person.

Family meals are where members share their daily lives.

All families have some dysfunctional characteristics, some more than others, and that's part of the human condition. The dysfunctional characteristics are passed on from generation to generation. But each generation can improve the system. There is always hope. No one member can directly change a family system, but if one member changes, he or she can influence the whole family system.

Having realistic expectations about one's family and a sense of commitment to that family prepares children to form their own families. They should know that there will always be tension between the urge to connect with a significant other and to be one's own person. It is only by engaging in continual communication and reasonable conflicts with the other that the tension can be kept in balance, as both the person and the relationship grow.

The family structure is further strengthened by the family's commitment to have family meals together. Family meals are where members share their daily lives, information is exchanged, and distortions corrected. The members of the family come to know one another and learn what is happening to each other. Communication at meals can lessen tension, diffuse conflict and anger, and heal hurts. Sometimes the atmosphere at a meal can become heated; sometimes disturbing issues are aired; sometimes laughter and lightheartedness surface, and joy and sorrows are shared. Indeed, the family meal, whether it involves dividing a pizza or indulging in a fine dinner, is the epicenter for the family's members to experience one another. More than food is shared: lives are also shared.

In today's hectic world, where families are caught up in multiple activities, with both parents working, planning family meals may be difficult. Parents will need to have a strong determination to organize family meals at least at some designated times of the week. Children may resist, so confident and convinced parents need to be consistent and firm in carrying out their plans. In the end families will benefit immensely from these family meals. The children will not only enjoy them, but will look forward to such gatherings. The meals will be remembered for years to come, as the children themselves follow these family meal traditions in their own families.

People's efforts to be home for family celebrations, especially at Thanksgiving and Christmas, gives ample evidence of the deep emotional importance that is attached to the family meal. It can be a spiritual experience which lifts people beyond the painful aspects of their lives, bringing healing and forgiveness, and keeping them united in good times and in bad.

Another binding force in the family is the commitment to share and express affirmation, approval, affection, appreciation, and gratitude. These fibers are intertwined to form a fiber that holds a family system together, even in the worst storms and tragedies. These characteristics—or rather, virtues—are frequently taken for granted and assumed to be part of the family, but unfortunately they are often missing. Adding to these virtuous characteristics are politeness and good manners, which are basic to self-respect and respect for others. Some people come by these qualities more naturally than others, but in either case, they must be developed and practiced or they will fade away.

The characteristics of a healthy family bring people out of themselves as they recognize others. They heal, bind, and foster intimacy. They bring a sense of belonging, of feeling worthwhile, and develop a sense of individuality. Members of the family realize their unique dignity. These virtues are often overlooked in families, or are considered secondary or only expressed to friends, when truly they are the foundation of a healthy, functioning family. Jesus sums it up well, "Where two or three are gathered together in my name there I am in their midst" (Matthew 18:20).

14.

Gratitude

Gratitude is a distinctive characteristic of a mature person and of an authentic Christian. Gratitude has a vision of God's goodness as it is manifested in all of the wonders of creation, in the history of the world, in our own lives, in our families, and in all people. Gratitude recognizes the realities of evil and injustice in the world, but is able to transcend these because gratitude always remembers the good. Gratitude generates the hope that good will always overcomes evil and that people, even though they are flawed, are basically good and gifted. Expressed gratitude is an essential aspect of all relationships, especially close ones. It bonds people together and heals wounded relationships.

A sure way of keeping a balance between our perception of the world around us and the harmony within our own lives is by being a

Gratitude brings peace to our hearts.

grateful person. Gratitude helps us keep good and evil in perspective, and not become myopic in our vision of life. It keeps our spirits buoyed while keeping our life's compass pointed in the correct direction, so that we can make adjustments when the storms of life blow us off course. Gratitude is an antidote to feelings of hopelessness and helplessness when we meet problems and tragedies. It energizes us with the courage to move forward.

Maintaining a grateful remembrance of the many gifts God has bestowed on us deepens our awareness of God's presence in our lives. It is disappointing and discouraging when people who have been blessed with so much remain bitter or angry, and turn from God when tragic and unfair events befall them. So often, after the initial shock of tragedy and loss, people become mired in grief, anger, and depression. They are not able to find a way to stabilize themselves and move on through the painful event.

Gratitude can't remove a painful disaster, but it can help us journey through the tragedy and the painful feelings in a balanced way. Gratitude recalls the good times of the past: successes, benefits, accomplishments, happy memories. Gratitude can restore hope, which engenders in us the ability to cope with present difficulties and with life's losses. Only an attitude of gratitude can bring some sanity into the midst of the madness around us. Gratitude assists us as we grieve over the many losses in our lives, and appreciate even more deeply the gifts and blessings we have enjoyed. Gratitude is part of the way we respond to life and its losses.

Gratitude was a major assistance for me as I grieved the recent death of my mother. Her noble qualities sharpened my sense of gratitude to God and to her and that played an important part in my ability to grieve over her loss. Gratitude is helping me through the sadness and other feelings I experienced at her passing.

We don't deny the presence of evil and suffering in life, but we don't allow them to overcome us. If they do, then we need to take responsibility for allowing them to overwhelm us and control our lives. We have the power within us to confront such situations.

Acknowledging and being grateful for this power strengthens our determination to cope.

Gratitude also keeps us balanced in our significant relationships. When we are hurt, we tend to focus on the wrong others inflicted, which in turn blocks out all the good and love they have shown us. Trying to recall their goodness and love and being thankful for them help us gradually to heal hurt and defuse anger while hastening forgiveness and reconciliation. Gratitude is not a magic wand, but it can be an asset as we try to stabilize our thinking, and a healing balm to our bruised spirit. Gratitude brings peace to our hearts and to the hearts of others. A simple "thank you" brings a smile to people's faces and gives us a sense of satisfaction.

When we express thanks to another we recognize their value; they feel worthwhile. Being grateful softens bitterness, lessens frustration, curbs impatience, and gladdens hearts. Such is the warmth and closeness people experience on Thanksgiving Day. Next to Christmas, this holiday is the most celebrated holiday in our country because Thanksgiving manifests the deep need that Americans have to express their gratefulness to one another and to God.

Everyone wants to be happy and deserves to find some degree of happiness in this life. Happiness is a characteristic that comes from within ourselves. We are responsible for its development. No one can give it to us. No one else can make us happy. People too frequently seek their happiness from others or from material goods. This is a major mistake that leads to endless frustrations.

Happy persons usually have a keener awareness of the goodness and blessings in their lives. Notice that the more grateful people are the happier they seem to be. They manifest contentment, satisfaction, and appreciation for the successes, goodness, and gifts that life brings them. Happiness breeds more happiness, but happiness is nourished by gratitude. "For happiness is not what makes us grateful. It is gratitude that makes us happy" (David Steindl-Rast).

Isn't it amazing how many people who seem to have everything are unhappy? They do not manifest a sense of gratitude that could influence their state of mind for good. Then there are those who have little but are happy because they are grateful for what they do have. The difference is an attitude of gratitude.

Some of our disturbing memories are of people for whom we did much good, whom we reached out to when they were in need, and to whom we were present in their distress. But perhaps they turned away from us when we may have failed them or offended them. Sometimes, it may have been an imagined hurt that they experienced. Where is the justice in all this? These people might now be rightfully hurt and angry—but what about the good they received from us in the past? Have these been forgotten? Shouldn't gratitude be a reason for mercy, compassion, and understanding? This experience can be very painful. Yet we never allow ourselves to be bitter because of such ingratitude. Rather, we should resolve to be more gracious, giving, and grateful persons.

Granted, being seriously offended by a friend may be enough to break a relationship, but we must never forget the good the other person did for us. This remembering can help us manage the hurt and anger we feel. Grateful memories need to be remembered as we mourn lost relationships.

One of the most frustrating persons we meet in life is the chronic complainer. He or she is never satisfied or at peace. For them, happiness is a lost art. The complainer is a card-carrying malcontent who thrives and is energized by being critical and negative. The glass is always half-empty. A grateful spirit is missing from their lives. They are anxious people and often suffer from deep wounds.

We can't allow ourselves to be infected by such people. We can prevent this illness from afflicting us, taking over our lives, and making us miserable persons by developing an attitude of gratitude.

Nourishing an Attitude of Gratitude

Here are some suggestions that can help you nourish an attitude of gratitude. First, be grateful for what you have. Often say thanks to others. Look on the bright side of life without denying the bad, the evil, and the unjust. Realize how well off you are. Broaden your vision of life by seeing the whole picture, the bad as well as the good. Keep things in perspective.

We must give praise and thanks to God in our daily lives, so we need to do the same with one another. Never assume that others realize we are grateful. We need to say "thanks" time and time again.

Others need to hear it. Gratitude is a source of bonding, healing, and affirming in all our relationships, especially in marriage and family.

Gratitude is learned first in the family.

The character of people can be determined by the presence or absence of gratitude in their lives and relationships. Gratitude that is expressed, that flows from the heart and soul, characterizes a mature person. This gratitude is expressed not only in words but by gracious, loyal, and faithful behavior.

The cornerstone of solid relationships is expressed gratitude, which manifests respect and regard for another. Gratitude helps us transcend the hurts we experience in marriages and families while transforming these relationships. Gratitude heals our wounds and the brokenness within our relationships and ourselves. Gratitude comforts us and brings a smile to us, lifts up our spirits, and may even bring us a greater sense of gratitude and generosity toward others. The simple words "thank you" have the power to transform people's lives.

Gratitude can also act as an antidepressant to stymie hopelessness and helplessness. By being appreciative for what we now have as well as for the many good things in our past, including the problems that we resolved, our spirits can be lifted up. All these positive thoughts and memories can promote optimism, which in turn strengthens our self-confidence and trust that God's presence is working in our lives.

We will never receive all the gratitude and appreciation we deserve. We need to have realistic expectations. This is especially important for people who are in the helping professions, and, above all, for parents. From my experience, there seems to be a greater degree of such ingratitude and insensitivity from children today than ever before. Parents sometimes fail to train their children to be grateful and to express gratitude. The attitude of gratitude is learned first in the family. Parents not only have to teach their children how to be grateful, they must express their own hurt and disappointment when the children are not grateful. Parents are not putting the children on a guilt trip when they do this, but sensitizing them to a very important aspect of healthy human relationships and Christian family living.

Today's parents are often criticized for over-indulging their children's desires for material goods. Sometimes this over-indulgence is the parents' way of making up for their own deprived childhood. Sometimes it is a compensation for their own lack of emotional and physical presence in their children's lives. In either case parents seem to retreat from asking for or expecting gratitude. Do they expect their children to be spontaneous about being grateful? Spontaneity comes after education and is rooted in consistent discipline.

Ultimately parents bear the responsibility of imbuing their children with a spirit of gratitude by their own words, teaching, and example. Gratitude will be significant characteristic of their children's personality. It will make a difference in their lives with regard to their emotional maturing, the quality of their relationships, and their perception of a gracious God. An attitude of gratitude improves the atmosphere of respect, sensitivity, and bonding in a family. Gratitude gives purpose for a family to worship God together on Sunday.

It bears repeating: an attitude of gratitude can transform us. As grateful persons, we become more gracious, generous, warm, and approving of others, less negatively critical, more appreciative for what we have, and more sensitive to the good that others do for us. We become more aware of and sensitive to the goodness in other people; and, above all, to the goodness, the love, the forgiveness, mercy, and compassion of the God who dwells among us and whom we call our Father.